GOD AND THE WORLD

GOD
AND
THE WORLD

by
JOHN B. COBB, JR.

THE WESTMINSTER PRESS
Philadelphia

STANDARD BOOK No. 664–24860–8

LIBRARY OF CONGRESS CATALOG CARD No. 69–11374

10 9 8 7 6

Published by The Westminster Press ®
Philadelphia, Pennsylvania

PRINTED IN THE UNITED STATES OF AMERICA

TO THE PROTESTANT THEOLOGICAL FACULTY
JOHANNES GUTENBERG UNIVERSITY
MAINZ, GERMANY
IN RESPECT AND GRATITUDE

When a book title connects two words with an "and," it can mean that both topics are treated or that the relation of the two is the unifying subject of the book. In this case the latter is intended. This is not a book about God, nor is it a book about the world. It is a book about how God is in the world and how the world is in and from God. The title points further to the major underlying thesis of the book. Against those who see us as being forced to choose God *or* the world, I am affirming that we must choose God *and* the world. To choose one against the other is in the end to reject both. Today there is a pervasive belief that the affirmation of the world and wholehearted involvement in it is the Christian's calling. This attitude has much to commend it. But it is sometimes presented as if a life oriented to the world were incompatible with devotion to God. Elsewhere we find the rejection of the world as a structured sociopolitical order in favor of the quest of the divine in religious or quasi-religious experience. My thesis is that when the affirmation of the world is cut off from faith in God, it ultimately undercuts itself, and that a devotion to the divine which turns its back upon the world is a rejection of the God known in Jesus Christ.

The reader will find the most direct treatment of this thesis in the final chapter. Except for the brief postscript, that chapter was written seven years earlier than any other part of the book. It is included because, despite the dated and over-simplified character of some of its points, it is my clearest statement of the conviction that underlies the whole book, the conviction that the vision of the world as creation is the context and presupposition of Christian belief and theology. This vision implies *both* the intrinsic importance of the world *and* its radical subordination to God. The importance of the world derives from its relation to God, and this relationship is such that faith in God expresses itself as the affirmation of the world and involvement in it. The burden of the chapter is the problem caused for Christian theology by the fading of the vision of the world as creation, a fading that initially had primarily intellectual causes.

The theme of creation is treated in a quite different light in Part I, which constitutes the latest writing in the book. In response to the recent vehement protests against the repressive character of Christian belief, I have recognized that the "Creator" imagery, when made central for the Christian understanding, *can* have, and all too often has had, repressive consequences. The reader will rightly sense a contrast between these three chapters and the final one. I believe the contrast is not a contradiction and that both points should stand. The Christian vision presupposes and embodies the Creator-creation relation (the emphasis of Chapter 6), but to be Christian it must view God's creative action in the light of what is revealed in Jesus Christ (the emphasis of Part I). Hence the Creator, for the Christian, must not be conceived as an all-determining potentate fashioning things according to his arbitrary will. Love, rather than compulsion, is God's mode of creative action. The fullest exposition of this point is in Chapter 4 on the subject of evil, for nothing more deeply challenges the vision of the world as creation than does the pervasive reality of misery and sin.

Chapter 5 is on the duality of the religious and the secular, rather than of God and the world. This is a different duality, but its close relation to the major theme of the book is obvious. In recent theology, "secular" has shifted from an all too pejorative word to an all too laudatory one. Theologians have differed as to whether becoming fully secular requires abandonment of belief in God. Paul van Buren thinks it does, whereas Schubert Ogden argues that true secularity requires faith in God rightly understood. My sympathies are basically with Ogden, but I have formulated the problem somewhat differently.

The essays included in this volume were selected partly for continuity of theme and partly for their nontechnical character. The latter criterion has led in each instance to the choice of material originally prepared for oral delivery or discussion rather than for publication. I have made a few deletions and revisions, but I have not tried to change the personal style of informal papers into the more impersonal one usual in publications. Nor have I introduced references and documentation except where this was absolutely necessary. Bibliographical data on these references will be found at the end of the book. I hope the result is readable and intelligible for those who are not specialists in theology.

Even so, the reader will not find the book altogether easy. It is written out of an understanding of reality informed chiefly by the philosophy of Alfred North Whitehead. That understanding differs profoundly from what many persons experience as common sense, a common sense that is too often taken as normative by contemporary philosophers and theologians. This common sense can accommodate neither the world of the physicist nor the world of Christian faith without extension and transformation. I hope this book can contribute something to that extension and transformation, but to do so it must inevitably make heavier demands on the reader than do books which accept the existing common sense and operate within it. These demands may be felt most keenly in Chapter 3, where philosophical issues are treated most explicitly. On the other hand, even Chapter 3 will not satisfy the critical reader. For his benefit I have included a few references to places where I have presented the underlying framework of thought more rigorously.

This book would not have been prepared apart from the invitation to deliver the Otts Lectures at Davidson College in February, 1968, and the encouragement to publish which is connected with that lectureship. I want to take this occasion to express my gratitude to the many persons at Davidson who made my visit there both memorable and pleasant. The first three chapters are in substance the lectures there presented.

Chapter 4 is taken from a paper, " Experienced Evil and the Power of God," written for a meeting of theologians which was part of the sesquicentennial celebration of Colgate Rochester Divinity School in September, 1967. Chapter 5 was prepared for the Pacific Coast Theological Group, which chose " Christianity as a Religion " as its topic for discussion in the fall of 1966. Chapter 6 was presented to a local Claremont discussion group in 1959.

For the content and context of the thought of this book my indebtedness to Whitehead and to my teacher, Charles Hartshorne, is pervasive. But their philosophical doctrines, even in the form in which I assimilated them in A Christian Natural Theology, do not altogether determine the way in which their religious and existential meanings are to be affirmed. In this respect, so far as I am aware, the ideas of Rudolf Bultmann, Wolfhart Pannenberg, and Thomas Altizer have played, positively and negatively, the largest roles in shaping my thought. I am aware also of the not inconsiderable influence of the preaching of my pastor, Pierce Johnson. Quotations and references in the text point to some of the other sources of the ideas offered.

My assistant, David Griffin, aided greatly in the preparation of the book. He read all the material and made numerous helpful suggestions for improvement. He is largely responsible for the selection from unpublished materials of the essays which make up Part II. His successor as my assistant, Delbert Swanson, has made additional improvements and checked the proof.

Thomas Altizer read much of the material and gave useful criticism and encouragement. Hartzell Cobbs, Richard

Knowles, and Marshall Osman also made helpful suggestions. In this respect as in others the staff of The Westminster Press has been unfailingly helpful.

The book is dedicated to the Protestant Faculty of the University of Mainz in appreciation for the surprising favor shown me in the awarding of an honorary degree. I was already in their debt for the hospitality extended to me and to my family in 1965–1966. I hope that I may in the future prove worthy of this gracious expression of their confidence.

J.B.C.

Claremont, California

CONTENTS

GOD AND THE WORLD

PART I. THE GOD OF JESUS AND THE GOD
WHO IS DEAD

Chapter
1

WHERE WE STAND

The central task of theology is the formulation of a
doctrine of God. This fact has often been obscured, and in the
past generation it sometimes seemed that man or history was
the major concern of theology. But the recent vigorous rejection of belief in God on the part of a few articulate theologians
has uncovered for us once again the absolute centrality of
this issue. If we cannot speak of God, then much of what we
have said about man and history turns out to be meaningless
or arbitrary.

In one sense, the question of the reality or unreality of
" God " *can* be settled by definition. That is, on the one hand,
it is possible to offer definitions of " God " which would lead
almost everyone to deny that any reality corresponded to the
term. For example, " God " could be defined as a being who
dwells above us beyond the skies and occasionally interferes
in events on this planet. If any clear meaning can be attached
to these words, almost all of us would assert the nonexistence

of such a being, and if no meaning can be assigned to these words, then the question of the existence of " God," in that sense, cannot even arise. On the other hand, we could define " God " as our name for the cause or causes of happiness. It would then be hard for anyone to deny that " God," in this sense, exists. There does seem to be such a thing as happiness, and most of us suppose that the occurrence of happiness has some cause or causes.

But, of course, serious debate about the existence of God is not settled in this way. Although we cannot prevent people from defining the word "God" in eccentric ways, there are central elements in its ordinary meaning. If these are omitted, the definition of " God " becomes private and arbitrary. For example, the word " God " normally and properly refers to *a unitary actuality which is supremely worthy of worship and/or commitment.* Atheism normally means the denial that there is any such unitary actuality. The atheist may, and often does, commit himself provisionally to many things, and he may be able to explain his commitments by pointing to some characteristic of all these things which elicits this commitment. He may work to increase human happiness in general through a variety of social and political agencies. But he does not understand " human happiness in general " as a unitary actuality. There are only individual instances of more or less happy people.

Although the definition of " God " as a unitary actuality supremely worthy of worship and commitment is sufficiently specific to make either an affirmation or a denial of God's existence meaningful, it is still quite formal, allowing for much leeway in giving a more definite idea of God. Different cosmologies and ontologies can supply further definiteness, as can divergent judgments of worth and importance. Furthermore, and of chief interest here, men are led to speak of God by different features of their experience, and thus they have different conceptions of God. Five such features have played prominent roles in the past.

Past theories:
Features of expl. these
WHERE WE STAND   what we conceive **21** of God

First, men have been led to speak of God by reflection on ①
the kind of unity which must be possessed by that *whole* of
which they and all that they know are tiny parts. Those who
conceive the parts as self-contained and self-explanatory units
and the whole simply as the sum total of the parts will not
speak of God, for such a whole has no unity of its own. But
those who see the parts as incomplete, as pointing beyond
themselves to ever more encompassing wholes for their explanation, may view the entirety, the universe or the cosmos,
as being that Whole in which and by which the parts have
their being. That Whole may well inspire them to worship
and commitment.

Men may also be led to speak of God through reflection on ②
the *order* they observe and which is revealed to them in in-
creasing intricacy by the advances of the sciences. Those who
understand such order as imposed by the human mind or as
the product of chance or as simply to be acknowledged without explanation will not speak of God. But those who find
themselves driven to seek a unified explanation for a unified
order may think in terms of cosmic mind or intelligent will,
and if so, they are likely to see in this unitary actuality that
which is of supreme worth.

A third possibility is that men may be led to speak of God
through their sense of *absolute dependence* for their existence ③
on something other than themselves. This mode of dependence
is not to be confused with that of an effect upon a cause in
the temporal sequence. It is rather the dependence of any element in the succession of causes and effects upon that which
gives it being or existence. It is the relation to what Tillich
called the Ground of being or the Power of being. It is the
creaturehood which can be philosophically described as radical contingency both of man and of the entire world.

Or men who are little moved by these cosmological and ontological considerations may yet in their *moral experiences* find ④
themselves confronted by an absolute " ought." Those who
understand this in the Freudian sense as superego or who re-

gard it as the conditioned product of their culture will see no reason to speak of God. But those who find that the " ought " has an ultimacy and an authority not explicable in these ways may experience it as embodying the will or demand of a transcendent Other. They may find that they owe to this Other worship and commitment and, hence, name it " God."

Or finally, men may be led to speak of God through more ⑤ distinctively *religious experience.* Rudolf Otto has shown us the universal character of experiences of the sacred, the holy, or the numinous. Such experiences could, of course, be explained psychologically without reference to an Other who is experienced. Yet, in the experience itself, the sense of the Other is very strong indeed. And those who have vivid experiences of this type may be led to name that Other " God."

I have said that men are led to speak of God by diverse features of their experience, and I have identified five ways in which this has occurred. Each of these approaches leads to a different view of God. But the term " God " need not for this reason name five different actual or supposed realities. It may be that one and the same reality is reached in all these ways, so that they are all compatible. The Whole may be the Source of order in nature, and this Source may also be the Power or Ground of our being. The Ground of being may be also the ultimate Ground of our moral obligation, and it may be this same reality which is encountered as the numinous. Hence, no one approach need *exclude* the others.

However, the beliefs that arise in the different approaches may be in *tension* with each other. For example, the man who knows God as that on which he, along with everything else, is absolutely dependent may be led by reflection on this situation to stress the otherness of God and the world, or God's radical transcendence of the world, and hence he may resist any attempt to equate God with the Whole of the world. Or the man who meets God in moral experience may draw the conclusion that God has nothing to do with nature and, hence, reject the view that God is also the Source of natural order. In such ways each of the five starting points for reflection about God tends to lead to a theological development somewhat different from the others, since each places emphasis on a different feature of human experience.

My own view is that the case for theism can be considerably strengthened if the mutual compatibility of all these grounds for belief is displayed in a single coherent doctrine of God and God's action in the world and in history. I am convinced that this can and should be done, and I have tried to contribute to this task elsewhere (e.g., in *A Christian Natural Theology*). Yet even if this is fully achieved, it will be insufficient for our need for at least four reasons.

First, these traditional ways of thinking about God have only a tenuous foothold in contemporary experience. The notion of the Whole is today confused by uncertainty over whether the universe is finite or infinite, and in any case the Whole seems so vast, so remote, so empty, and so indifferent that it is difficult for the spark of the sense of being part of the Whole to be fanned into religious fervor. Similarly, the notion of order in the natural sciences has become so complex and so subject to dispute that it offers little foothold for a leap beyond it to its Source. Again, although the sense of absolute dependence is not totally lacking in the modern consciousness, it plays no prominent role. Christians may believe that the fact that we derive our being from God leaves an imprint on experience such that others should be able to respond with recognition when this thought is emphasized, but the interest in this dimension of experience is slight and the ability to uncover it weak. Further, the moral " ought " has become in the popular mind bound up with mores, especially in the field of sex, that are fully recognized as culturally conditioned and are not even felt as appropriate for our own culture; so the close association of God with the sense of obligation is exceedingly problematic. And finally, our culture in general has become so secular that most men screen out the religious dimensions of experience. Only in certain subcultures is there keen interest in the experience of the holy or sacred, and there the desired experiences are often achieved by drugs or other artificial means in such a way that the question of their source or object is extremely confused.

This does not mean that it is impossible to argue for the reality of God in the traditional ways. But whereas in the past the starting points for such argumentation were readily accessible in widespread human experience, today it is difficult to bring such starting points to consciousness. We may be grateful that some men are devoting themselves to this task. If traditional Christian belief in God were challenged only because of the weakness of the evidence to which it appeals, this would be the chief task of the apologist. But because there are other even more serious challenges to the traditional doctrine, we will proceed instead to consider these and the problems raised by them.

The second reason for the inadequacy of traditional thought about God is that it is not distinctively or centrally Christian. That does not mean that Christians should abandon the five approaches to God described above. To some extent they are presupposed by the New Testament or can and should be presupposed by later theology. Nevertheless, it is odd and even shocking that Christians have so often taken aspects of experience that are not prominent in the New Testament as their *essential* clues to the identification of that which is supremely worthy of worship and commitment. Furthermore, when what is treated as the essential clue to thinking about God arises in experience that is not distinctively Christian, it should not surprise us if the total doctrine of God which follows, even when it tries to take account of uniquely Christian revelation, remains somewhat alien to the Christian gospel.

This second objection to traditional theology is presented here briefly so that we may proceed to fuller discussion of the third and fourth. Nevertheless, it not only provides a reason for penitence for our past failure but also suggests that there may be a way out of our present difficulties. Perhaps by think-

ing of God in a more fully Christian way we will also find that
we will reduce, or even remove, the force of the objections to
faith in God on the part of those who have rejected it. (This
is the theme of Chapter 2.)

The third difficulty with the traditional understanding of
God is that it does not square with the experienced evil in the
world. The problem of evil has long been regarded as an *intellectual* puzzle generated by the twin claims that God is all-
good and all-powerful in conjunction with the fact of evil. If
God could prevent this evil and does not, so the argument
runs, then he is not entirely good; and if he cannot prevent it,
then he is not all-powerful.

Philosophers and theologians have produced numerous re-
plies to these objections. They have argued that the evils in
the world in one way or another make possible greater goods
and that where this possibility for greater good is not realized,
the fault lies with man's sin rather than with God's purposes.
But this kind of answer has become increasingly ineffective in
the twentieth century. Modern man is sure this is not the best
possible world because in limited but important ways he has
himself been able to improve it. We can see our elimination of
certain diseases as a distinct possibility, and from this perspective the question as to why God allowed these diseases to rav-
age mankind for all these centuries cannot be answered by
appeal to some overall harmony or perfection of the whole.
Nor can one believe the presence of these diseases to be justified as a challenge to man's ingenuity, since plenty of such
challenges remain. Nor can they reasonably be viewed as punishment, since it would be strange if a divinely imposed punishment could be removed by man's efforts. The realities of
our human situation do not seem to fit with the belief in the
traditional conception of God as omnipotent Creator and Lord
of history.

Even if an intellectual reconciliation of the goodness of an
almighty deity with the evil in the world were achieved, the
problem would not be removed. The problem is an existential

one as well, and in the name of solidarity with a suffering humanity a man may revolt against the Creator–Lord of history. The problem of evil in the unity of its cognitive and existential dimensions has never been put more powerfully than by Albert Camus in his novel *The Plague*. The priest and the doctor represent what Camus understands as respectively the Christian and the humanist responses. The priest calls for repentance and resignation. The doctor will not believe in a God who sends plagues, but he sees a job to be done in the relief of human suffering. There is hardly one of us who does not side with the doctor, especially as we stand with him at the bedside of a boy in agony.

With equal poignancy Richard Rubenstein tells us in *After Auschwitz* that he as a Jew can no longer believe in a Lord of history. Believers in such a Lord have been compelled to see in every historical calamity a meaning derived from God's inclusive purposes. But a purpose that could justify Hitler's genocide can only be evil. If history has this kind of Lord, he is to be rejected.

Both Camus and Rubenstein turn away from what they understand to be the Biblical God to the gods of nature. Camus returns to the Mediterranean sun and the human body; Rubenstein, to the gods of the Palestinian soil. They turn away from the traditional God of the West because they find it necessary to regard him as responsible for inexcusable evil.

An alternative response to the honest recognition of the reality and scope of evil is to come to a new understanding of God's power. H. Richard Niebuhr in *The Meaning of Revelation* called attention to the surprising way in which God's power is " made manifest in the weakness of Jesus, in the meek and dying life which through death is raised to power. . . . [God's] power is made perfect in weakness and he exercises sovereignty more through crosses than through thrones " (p. 187).

John Dillenberger has made still more explicit than Niebuhr the full extent to which Christians have failed to rethink God's power in the light of revelation. He recognizes that Karl Barth,

for example, intends to describe God's attributes in the light
of revelation, but he sees that even Barth has not gone far
enough in this direction. Dillenberger writes:

> More needs to be said than that the traditional attri-
> butes have continued too long under the aegis of general
> philosophical notions. We must see the full scope of the
> distortion in the traditional views. The general notions
> of the omnipotence and omniscience of God define power
> and knowing in ways that are actually analogous to
> what sinful man would like to be able to do and know
> were he himself God. Sinful man would like to have all
> power to eliminate the problems that frustrate him and
> the world, and to know all things — past, present, and
> future. But it may be that God's omnipotence is the love
> by which he does not need to have such an arrogating
> power and that God's knowing of man is such that he
> can be open to the frustrating and joyful dynamics of
> the future. (*The New Hermeneutic*, p. 158.)

My own contribution to the reconception of God's power
will be found below in Chapter 4. But before developing this
response to the challenge of such men as Camus and Rubenstein, we need to consider the still more fundamental association of God and evil raised by the fourth objection to classical theism.

This fourth objection is that faith in God actually operates
against the attainment of full humanity. This objection is directed especially against images of God derived chiefly from
the Old Testament, such as those of Creator, Lord of history,
Lawgiver, Judge, and the One who alone is holy. But when
God is apprehended in the five ways considered above, these
images tend to be reinforced. Indeed, these approaches themselves have led in the West to a conceptuality that is largely a
philosophical or secularized formulation of the vivid Old Tes-

tament imagery. (Both in the five approaches that have been discussed and in the process of philosophical reformulation of Biblical concepts, the influence of Greek philosophy, and especially of the idea of perfection as involving immutability, impassibility, and timelessness, has been important. But exposition of the complex ways in which Christian theism has been influenced by its Greek heritage would distract from the main point of this chapter.)

The understanding of God as the Source of order and Ground of being is closely related to the Old Testament understanding of him as Creator and Lord of history, and even the approach to God as the Whole has tended to reinforce a similar sensibility, for example, in the influential thought of Spinoza. This approach to God suggests that men are powerless in his hands, since they depend upon him for all that they are. It evokes the responses of awe, obeisance, self-abnegation, and resignation. It is thus in tension with the view that men have dignity in themselves. It is in tension also with the concern that men accept more radical responsibility for themselves and their societies and that they work against injustice and oppression.

The understanding of God as Creator and Lord of history, or as Source of order and Ground of being, *need* not have these existential consequences, and it is found in theologians who draw quite different conclusions. But when it is taken as the *key* to the understanding of God, it tends to have these results in the sensitive imagination. To the extent to which these consequences are effective, God is experienced as the enemy of man's claims to dignity and of his desire to assume responsibility for himself.

The idea that God is encountered in the moral " ought " or the categorical imperative is the secularized version of the Biblical understanding of God as Lawgiver and Judge. It suggests that the ground and content of obligation are outside of man, over against him, pressing down upon him. His wishes and opinions cannot stand before the divine demand. This implies that man's proper role is to suppress his own perceptions and judgments and simply acquiesce to those which are imposed upon him.

The understanding of God as Lawgiver and Judge *can* be so developed that this repressive character is avoided. But when moral obligation is made the central clue in man's experience for his understanding of God, such repression tends to result. To whatever extent this is the case, God functions in the modern consciousness as the enemy of man's efforts to become whole and free.

Finally, the correlation of the diffuse sense of the sacred with the Old Testament understanding of Yahweh as the Holy One of Israel is obvious. In our secularized age, Tillich has shown that the sense of the sacred is more apparent to us in the realization that there is a dimension of *ultimacy* in our concerns. For the Western sensibility, the close connection of the sense of the sacred or of the ultimate with the Holy One of Israel functions to distance God from man and the world, to confirm his radical trancendence of the world, and to stress that God is " wholly other " to us and to all else that we know. Thus, where the ultimate or sacred is the crucial element in the understanding of God, and everything else is seen as profane, God so absorbs meaning and value into himself as to drain all else of significance. Modern man, who can only understand himself and his world in profane terms, thus finds himself and his world denied all value and even reality.

The understanding of God as the Holy One does not have to have this effect upon the believer. Indeed, it did not have this effect for most of Hebrew experience. In Biblical literature this effect appears only in apocalypticism. Yet precisely this apocalypticism expresses the deepest meaning and the culmination of a major element of Hebrew experience. When God is understood essentially as the holy, sacred, or numinous, the resultant polarization of value and importance is to the detriment of the secular. We see this also in some elements of the hippie community, which seek the ultimate intensities of experience and lose interest in the mundane particularities of business, family, and citizenship. In this way, too, God as the Holy One can function in the experience of modern man as the enemy of reflective rationality, calculating prudence, and commitment to the intermediate goals on which civilization and historical progress depend.

We have been considering five ways in which men have been led to speak of God and noting the tendency of these approaches to emphasize man's dependency, impotence, sinfulness, and worthlessness. To believe in God is often to disparage man and his capacities, to resign oneself to what occurs as good despite its apparent evil, and to repress one's spontaneity and vital feelings in obedience to an external demand.

I have repeatedly noted that the same cognitive understanding of God that has tended to have these results is susceptible to, and has also had, other quite different existential meanings for man. The understanding of God as the Whole can lead to the sense of participation in the divine Being. Knowing God as the Source of order has led to a faith in pattern and meaning behind the apparent disorder and meaninglessness of phenomena — a faith that has helped make the sciences possible. Experiencing God as Ground of being has undergirded the conviction that the world and its history matter ultimately because they matter to God. The awareness of God as confronted in moral experience has given man a sense of his uniqueness and dignity as a moral being who thereby transcends nature and is capable of fellowship with God. The experience of God as the one Holy One has served to empty the world of numinous terror and free man to conquer and to rule it. In these and other ways the understanding of God as Creator, Lord of history, Lawgiver, Judge, and Holy One has served to ennoble and free man as well as to restrict and repress him.

Furthermore, even the negative import of man's experience of God should not be entirely condemned. Men have a strong tendency, not less today than in earlier times, to exaggerate their virtues, rights, and powers; and it is wholesome that we be reminded of our fallibility, finitude, and sinfulness. Nevertheless, the Christian who is made aware of the extent to which his understanding of God has operated against man's fullest and most responsible development, cannot continue simply to speak of God in the old way.

The one who has taught us this lesson most effectively is Dietrich Bonhoeffer. He saw that the age-old attempt to persuade man of his need for God by pointing to man's limits as manifest in guilt and death has operated against man's maturation. It has associated belief in God with man's weakness and failure, trying to drive man to his knees and return him to the dependency of childhood. Now that man has come of age, this approach in the name of Christianity is both futile and wrong. Mature man has no need of this kind of God, which Bonhoeffer associated with religion.

Bonhoeffer's words have had peculiar power and poignancy because of the circumstances under which they were written. If they had been written in a time of peace, progress, and prosperity by one surrounded by the finest products of human wisdom and kindness, they could have been dismissed as the naïve optimism of one unacquainted with the depths of human sin and wretchedness and insensitive to the meaning of death. But Bonhoeffer wrote from a prison in Nazi Germany, where human depravity in its most obvious forms had gained control of Europe's greatest power, where death rained nightly from the Berlin skies, and where he was under constant threat of his own execution for his part in a plot against Hitler's life.

If the word "God" is unqualifiedly identified with this "religious" God against which Bonhoeffer speaks, then we can understand those who urge his total rejection. This is the position of Thomas Altizer, who believes that the word "God" points us to the sacred perceived as transcendent power and primordial authority. Altizer calls on us to *will* the death of God. He is not blind to the fact that meaningful existence in the West has been bound up with belief in this God and that his death hurls us into a void. But he proclaims the necessity of our entering this void and the hope that the extreme of its darkness will become a new light.

Since for Altizer the sacred known as Creator–Lord of history–Lawgiver–Judge *is* God, he calls his rejection " atheism." Yet he differs profoundly from Camus and Rubenstein in that he continues to identify himself as a Christian. Altizer's atheism is poles removed from the widespread positivistic, humanistic, and cynical atheisms of our day, for he proclaims atheism in the name of Christ. He sees the incarnate Word as that which calls us to give up our bondage to the past, to established law, to longing for return to innocence, and he urges us instead to turn wholeheartedly to the radically profane world which is given to us, which is always also the unknown future. This Christ or incarnate Word is not simply to be identified with Jesus or with any empirically specifiable phenomenon; rather, it is divine, redemptive Reality, conceived as wholly immanent in history. One can view Altizer's heresy, in traditional language, as Sabellianism, the doctrine that the persons of the Trinity are chronologically successive, such that the Father is replaced by the Son who is succeeded by the Holy Spirit. For Altizer as for the twelfth-century theologian, Joachim of Fiore, we live in the age of the Son and look forward to the coming of the third and final age — that of the Holy Spirit. In these terms, that against which Altizer inveighs with passion is our failure to give up in the age of the Son the imaginative and existential life appropriate only to the age of the Father, thereby refusing to move forward to the age of the Spirit.

When Altizer is viewed in this light, his own continued use of language about the divine in a positive sense becomes intelligible, and the deeply Christian character of his thought is apparent. We can view him in traditional language as having identified " God " with the first Person of the Trinity, the Almighty Father. Nor should we regard this as a strange aberration on his part, for this identification has been largely effected by almost the entire tradition. The classical creeds and their orthodox interpretations could do justice to the deity of the Son only by assimilating him to the Father — and not the intimate Father of Jesus' prayers but the awesome Father of the mythical and metaphysical imagination. In the end the Son's incarnation became no more intelligible than the Father's, and this was acknowledged in the doctrine that in fact the entire Trinity, now understood much as the first Person was originally understood, was incarnate in Jesus. In such a view the Person of Jesus ceases to function as a norm for the understanding of God — even for the understanding of the Son! The reign of the holy Creator–Lord of history–Lawgiver–Judge was renewed, hardly affected by the dogmatic assertion that he had once been incarnate. For Altizer this perversion of Christian faith is expressed in the doctrines of Resurrection and Ascension.

Perhaps only by unequivocally identifying God with the Father and calling for his replacement by the incarnate Word or Christ could Altizer break open to us the urgency of radical reconception and provide an adequate Christian interpretation of the spiritual crisis of our age. For this purpose it was necessary for him to risk total misunderstanding, and we should be grateful to him for having taken this risk. Only when we have realized intellectually as well as in the depths of our sensibility both the impossibility of the continued reign of the Almighty Father in the contemporary vision of reality *and* that the rejection of that reign is of the essence of Christian faith, can we authentically claim the future for Christ or, as I prefer, the God revealed in Jesus.

No theological formulation of our time has surpassed the power of Altizer's. Although I affirm a theistic form of Christian faith, my chastened and deepened appreciation of theism is indebted to Altizer's atheism.

When we view Altizer as a Christocentric thinker attacking an understanding of God that has obscured the character and claim of Christ, we can see him not so much in opposition to modern theology, but, rather, in its vanguard. Consider, for example, the most influential theologian of the twentieth century, Karl Barth. He originally made his reputation by powerfully reaffirming against historicistic, immanental, and humanistic tendencies of nineteenth-century liberalism the transcendent, wholly other, sovereign God of high Calvinism. But Barth from the beginning was concerned with the one revelation of God in Jesus Christ. Methodologically his position can be characterized as Christomonism; that is, he insisted that we know God *only* in this revelation. And this methodological insistence gradually altered the content of his doctrine of God. Seeing this, Gerrit Berkouwer wrote an excellent book entitled *The Triumph of Grace in the Theology of Karl Barth;* Barth himself published an essay on " The Humanity of God." Increasingly it became clear that God's Word to man is only Yes! and that this Word is addressed to man as man and hence to all men. Yet in Barth himself the full radicality of the Christomonism to which his development pointed has remained obscured by other themes in his doctrine of God.

A recent book by Dietrich Ritschl, *Memory and Hope: An Inquiry Concerning the Presence of Christ,* carries the thrust of Barthian thought further. For Ritschl, Augustine is the villain of Christian theology. It was Augustine who fatefully separated the understanding of God and that of Jesus. He synthesized and identified the God of Neoplatonism with that of the Bible and depicted the human situation fundamentally in relation to *that* God. He then interpreted the nature and work of Christ in a quite secondary way in terms of that situation. Ritschl proposes that the object of Christian faith and worship is *Christus praesens,* the Christ who is present to the congregation *now* because he is remembered and hoped for. For Ritschl, Father and Holy Spirit are subsumed into *Christus praesens,* and the fundamental direction of Christian attention is forward to the fulfillment of the remembered promises.

Freedom from the past and openness to the future, which for Altizer is virtually equivalent to the rejection of God in favor of the Word, is a familiar motif in recent theology. Rudolf Bultmann, our century's greatest New Testament scholar, recovered this for our whole generation as the meaning both of Jesus' message and of the Christian gospel. In faith we are set free from our past and made open to whatever new reality comes to us in each moment. *Bultmann*

The limitation that has been more recently felt in Bultmann's thought is the lack of hope. Openness to the future is openness to whatever future there may be, but Bultmann cannot appropriate the full optimism of the New Testament. For him the expectation of an earthly future radically different from the " now " we know is mythological and hence unacceptable.

Meanwhile, Marxists continued to affirm just such a future — the classless society to which history is carrying us by dialectical material processes. In orthodox Marxist formulations such a vision has largely lost its power. It supposes that man's spiritual condition is a by-product of his economic condition and that man's hunger for meaning and truth make no autonomous demands upon the future. But in the heretical and humanistic form of Marxism expounded by Ernst Bloch, especially in his *Das Prinzip Hoffnung*, hope for a transformed future effectively challenged a generation of Christian thinkers. The result has been a veritable explosion of future-oriented theology hardly less radical than Altizer's except in the decision to retain the word " God " and to stress continuities rather than discontinuities with the history of Christian thought. *Bloch*

Consider, for example, the theology of Wolfhart Pannenberg. He also maintains that faith is to be directed only toward the God revealed in Jesus and that this God is to be contrasted with the God of traditional theism. Pannenberg believes that existence in any moment is determined by its relation to the future. It derives meaning from this relation and its very content is dependent on its anticipation of what is to come. Ultimately, what is consciously or unconsciously anticipated is *Pannenberg* fulfillment. The Biblical image of this fulfillment is the Kingdom of God, and Pannenberg believes that the thrust of Jesus' message identifies God with the Kingdom of God. Thus, the locus of God is not past or present but future. He is that which is to be.

It is important to see that for Pannenberg this doctrine of God as future does not make God causally dependent on our activities or simply unreal or ineffective in the present. On the contrary, God as the Power of the future is the Ground of being and meaning in the present as he has been of every past. God is not now extant in the sense of being a Being alongside the other beings or a metaphysical Ground of being that stands eternally outside of time. But as the Power of the future he is already and always *the* power which empowers all other powers.

Pannenberg's thought differs sharply from that of Altizer in that he attributes to the Kingdom of God in its relation to our present many of the attributes Christians have in the past attributed to God the Father. He can speak, for example, of the omnipotence of God. Yet this difference is not so great as it seems. The sense in which the future determines the present through the phenomenon of anticipation is profoundly different from the traditional views of God's infinite power exerted upon the world from above, against which so much of contemporary theology has reacted.

To display the wide prevalence of an understanding of Christianity in terms of future-directed hope, we have only to list such additional names as Pierre Teilhard de Chardin, Leslie Dewart, and Johannes Metz among Roman Catholics and Gerhard Sauter, Jürgen Moltmann, and Harvey Cox among Protestants. These men differ markedly from one another, but all of them call us to live toward a future which has the character of fulfillment, and all of them see this mode of life as faithful to Christ. The God whose death Altizer urges us to will is for all of them displaced from centrality if not wholly dead. The God whom they continue to affirm is hardly to be distinguished either from Altizer's incarnate Word or from that new Reality for which Altizer hopes and to which we have given the name Holy Spirit.

The current preoccupation with the future may well be one-sided. Reactions usually are, and the current reaction against preoccupation with the Wholly Other transcendent Father, on the one hand, and the present existential moment, on the other, is no exception. But what should now be clear to all and what constitutes the thesis of this chapter is that *Christian faith is not essentially bound up with the God who is seen primarily as Creator–Lord of history–Lawgiver–Judge* and who has so long dominated the Christian sensibility and the imagination of the West. What the Christian knows in Jesus is something quite different, and something which speaks more of human responsibility than of total dependence, more of full humanity than of repression, more of hope than of nostalgia or fear. The One who is met in Jesus is the God who suffers with us and for us more than the God who demands and judges from on high. We may name him Christ with Altizer and Ritschl or we may continue to speak also of God as do the New Testament and the Christian tradition, but we must now, as never before, *allow what appeared in Jesus to give meaning and content to the Reality we thereby name.*

Perhaps if we turn to the New Testament for the clue to the understanding of this Reality, we will find a way to think of God that is not only Christian but also credible in the face of the evil in the world, that will make faith for us a source of strength and hope and an encouragement to maturity and responsibility. Perhaps the God who is revealed in Jesus will fulfill rather than repress the ideals and longings of the modern sensibility. Perhaps faith in this God will appear as the fullest humanization of man.

Bonhoeffer, to whom I have already referred as having taught the Christian church the wrongness of its older way of relating God to man's weakness, has also pointed us to the positive, if revolutionary, implications of taking the New Tes-

tament seriously as the basis for thinking about God. In one
of his letters he wrote:

> God allows himself to be edged out of the world and on
> to the cross. God is weak and powerless in the world, and
> that is exactly the way, the only way, in which he can
> be with us and help us. Matthew 8.17 makes it crystal
> clear that it is not by his omnipotence that Christ helps
> us, but by his weakness and suffering.
> This is the decisive difference between Christianity
> and all religions. Man's religiosity makes him look in his
> distress to the power of God in the world; he uses God as
> a *Deus ex machina*. The Bible however directs him to
> the powerlessness and suffering of God; only a suffering
> God can help. To this extent we may say that the process
> we have described by which the world came of age was
> an abandonment of a false conception of God, and a
> clearing of the decks for the God of the Bible, who con-
> quers power and space in the world by his weakness. This
> must be the starting point for our "worldly" interpreta-
> tion. (*Prisoner for God*, p. 164.)

Bonhoeffer wrote this on July 16, 1944. We may assume
that he wrote without knowledge of the somewhat similar
words of Alfred North Whitehead fifteen years earlier, near
the end of his major work, *Process and Reality*:

> The notion of God as the "unmoved mover" is de-
> rived from Aristotle, at least so far as Western thought
> is concerned. The notion of God as "eminently real" is
> a favourite doctrine of Christian theology. The combina-
> tion of the two into the doctrine of an aboriginal, emi-
> nently real, transcendent creator, at whose fiat the world
> came into being, and whose imposed will it obeys, is the
> fallacy which has infused tragedy into the histories of
> Christianity and of Mahometanism.

When the Western world accepted Christianity, Caesar conquered; and the received text of Western theology
was edited by his lawyers. The code of Justinian and the
theology of Justinian are two volumes expressing one
movement of the human spirit. The brief Galilean vision
of humility flickered throughout the ages, uncertainly. In
the official formulation of the religion it has assumed the
trivial form of the mere attribution to the Jews that they
cherished a misconception about their Messiah. But the
deeper idolatry, of the fashioning of God in the image of
the Egyptian, Persian, and Roman imperial rulers, was
retained. The Church gave unto God the attributes which
belonged exclusively to Caesar.

In the great formative period of theistic philosophy,
which ended with the rise of Mahometanism, after a con-
tinuance coeval with civilization, three strains of thought
emerge which, amid many variations in detail, respectively fashion God in the image of an imperial ruler, God
in the image of a personification of moral energy, God
in the image of an ultimate philosophical principle.
Hume's *Dialogues* criticize unanswerably these modes of
explaining the system of the world.

The three schools of thought can be associated respectively with the divine Caesars, the Hebrew prophets, and
Aristotle. But Aristotle was antedated by Indian, and
Buddhistic, thought; the Hebrew prophets can be paralleled in traces of earlier thought; Mahometanism and the
divine Caesars merely represent the most natural, obvious, theistic idolatrous symbolism, at all epochs and
places.

The history of theistic philosophy exhibits various
stages of combination of these three diverse ways of en-
tertaining the problem. There is, however, in the Galilean
origin of Christianity yet another suggestion which does
not fit very well with any of the three main strands of
thought. It does not emphasize the ruling Caesar, or the

ruthless moralist, or the unmoved mover. It dwells upon the tender elements in the world, which slowly and in quietness operate by love; and it finds purpose in the present immediacy of a kingdom not of this world. Love neither rules, nor is it unmoved; also it is a little oblivious as to morals. It does not look to the future; for it finds its own reward in the immediate present. (*Process and Reality*, pp. 519–521.)

Both Bonhoeffer and Whitehead reject the God of much tradition Western piety for many of the same reasons as does Altizer. Bonhoeffer rejects the "religious" understanding of God, which makes man "look in his distress to the power of God in the world." Whitehead writes with a passion hardly less than Altizer's against "the doctrine of an aboriginal, eminently real, transcendent creator, at whose fiat the world came into being, and whose imposed will it obeys." Against these traditional aspects of Christian theology Bonhoeffer appeals to the New Testament, Whitehead to the Galilean origin of Christianity. Neither opposes Christ to God as does Altizer, but both demand a revolutionary shift in the understanding of God in the name of what is distinctively Christian. That Bonhoeffer and Whitehead continue to speak of God while Altizer proclaims atheism is not a major issue between them. For all of them the holy, omnipotent Creator–Lord of history–Lawgiver–Judge must be superseded. Bonhoeffer speaks of God's weakness, powerlessness, and suffering. Whitehead speaks of the "tender elements in the world, which slowly and in quietness operate by love." Altizer might affirm the God of Bonhoeffer and Whitehead by naming him "Christ." Alternately, as I prefer, in the spirit of Bonhoeffer and Whitehead we can name the Christ of Altizer "God" without requiring that Altizer abandon the chief thrust of his message. (The issue of God's locus in the present [e.g., Bonhoeffer] or the future [e.g., Pannenberg] will be treated in the next chapter.)

In this chapter we have reviewed the ways in which West-

ern man has most often been led to think of God. We have
noted that these grounds of belief in God have lost much of
their persuasiveness for us. We have seen that despite the
Christian doctrine that God is revealed in Jesus Christ, the
basic understanding of God has been determined by other factors in thought and experience. We have seen also that many
moderns have been driven to blame the God so understood for
inexcusable evils in nature and history. And finally we have
found that God viewed in this way has functioned all too often
against the full maturation of man. In the light of all this it
appears that faith in God must and will be abandoned altogether unless the Christian radically reconceives God in the
light of the revelation he has always affirmed.

The philosophical conceptuality that underlies my thought
comes from Whitehead, and I will try to communicate this
more directly in the third chapter. But in the next chapter I
want to describe how I as a Christian involved in and moved
by the currents of thought of our time have come to think of
God. Just as the people joined in the ancient cry on the death
of a king, "The king is dead; long live the king!" so I want
to join the chorus that today is proclaiming, "God is dead;
long live God!"

Chapter
2

THE ONE WHO CALLS

In the first chapter, I presented an emerging consensus in contemporary Christian thought. This consensus is largely a negative one, agreeing that the God of much traditional Christian theism is dying and deserves to die. The consensus is positive insofar as it appeals against this kind of classical theism to the Reality known to us in Jesus Christ.

The historically recoverable happening that we call Jesus Christ is a complex one involving Jesus' own message, his impact on others both during his lifetime and through his death and resurrection appearances, and the church's reflection upon his meaning. Neither this reality as a whole nor any aspect of it can be simply transplanted into our day. All who appeal to Jesus Christ as the clue to a contemporary Christian reconception of God necessarily do so by selection and translation, guided by judgments about our own situation. The historical material speaks to us with sufficient clarity to enable us to judge that some conceptions of God which have paraded as

Christian have been fundamentally false to the meaning of Jesus Christ. But the selections and the translations lead to a sometimes confusing diversity.

Such differences were illustrated in the previous chapter, where it was noted that Bonhoeffer speaks of God as weak and suffering, while Whitehead refers to the tender elements in the world which work by love. Both appealed to Jesus Christ in the broad sense in which we are here understanding that reality, but their selections and translations differ. However, in this instance the issue raised by the diversity is not serious. Although Whitehead rejects the view that God is literally lacking in all forms of power, other statements of Bonhoeffer make clear that he did not mean to be understood so strictly. The two men share the rejection of God as an omnipotent monarch interfering to benefit his favorites. Furthermore, in his comprehensive position Whitehead undergirds Bonhoeffer's intuitive theological assertions about the suffering of God.

While Whitehead and Bonhoeffer are, if one considers the contrasting traditions in which they stand, remarkably compatible, there are other differences among recent thinkers which cannot be so easily reconciled. The intense focus of attention upon the future, characteristic of much contemporary theology and bound up with its understanding of Jesus Christ, is foreign to both Whitehead and Bonhoeffer. Neither the God who works slowly and quietly by love nor the God who helps us by his suffering can be readily identified with Pannenberg's Power of the future. Both Whitehead and Bonhoeffer, along with Bultmann, call us out of our bondage to the past into the full reality of the present and openness to whatever the future may bring. But the meaning of the present does not depend upon hope for a radically different future. It is found for Bonhoeffer in sharing now in the sufferings of God in the world, for Whitehead "in the present immediacy of a kingdom not of this world."

The question of the relation of present and future is in the center of the contemporary discussion, and in part this discussion is about how Jesus himself understood this relation. At one extreme is the view that he was an apocalypticist announcing the imminent coming of the resurrection of the dead as an event altogether discontinuous with all history including his own ministry. At the other extreme is the view that Jesus focused attention primarily upon the new work of God which was beginning already in his teaching and healing and in the table fellowship with the disciples. Most scholars find it unnecessary to choose between these extremes, believing that they can do justice to both the future and the present as emphases in Jesus' message. Without seeking to solve the important historical issues that are here at stake, we can make a few general statements about Jesus and his teaching which are widely acceptable and which suffice for our immediate purposes.

The message of Jesus, proclaimed in word and deed, was the coming of the Kingdom of God. That coming Jesus saw as already realized in his power over demons and in his table fellowship with sinners. That coming he also expected as the consummation of all things in the imminent future. Both as present and as future the Kingdom of God represented for Jesus a sharp break with the past.

The Judaism of Jesus' day associated God primarily with its national life and institutions. God was viewed as the transcendent authority whose past acts sanctioned the inherited way of life and forbade its alteration. On the other hand, Jesus' way of announcing the coming Kingdom implied quite a different understanding of God. Instead of sanctioning received institutions and laws, God is he whose coming puts an end to their authority. Thus, even in the present, all that is inherited from the past appears as of only relative or provisional value in the light of the new action of God.

For Jesus, to know God was not to intensify obedience to ancient laws; it was to be free from bondage to such laws. To respond to God was to give up the security of habitual, customary, and socially approved actions and to live in terms of a radically new and uncontrollable future. The present moment

Not so unlike
Heb. scriptures as he
claims.

was always a time for a decision required by the coming of the new reality and made possible by the radical forgiveness of all that was past.

These comments on the locus of God in the message of Jesus serve to explain the contemporary consensus that classical theism has too often embodied an understanding of God quite different from that of Jesus. This theism has tended to confront us with the God who sanctions norms and institutions established in the past rather than the God who calls us into the new future. Instead of seeking God through the sense of the Whole, of absolute dependence, of order, of obligation, and of the holy, the Christian will be in greater continuity with Jesus if he seeks God in the call to go forward beyond the achievements of the past and the security of what is established and customary.

Of course, the modern Christian must always recognize that in this approach, as in any other, a great distance separates his experience and conceptuality from Jesus. We cannot go back to Jesus if that would mean simply repeating his beliefs. We can only go forward in a way that somehow corresponds for our time to the meaning of his life and message for the men of his time. My proposal is that we can do this best by attending to what I am hereafter designating as the *call forward*.

Our task now is to consider this call forward more closely. The following pages will pursue this task, beginning with an analysis of the call as an aspect of experience and moving to consideration of the kind of objectivity possessed by that which calls and to the possibility that " that which calls " may be also " One Who Calls." The following three questions will be treated in succession:

1. Can we identify the call forward in our experience as something distinctive?

2. If we can, does this call direct us beyond itself to something which calls?

3. If it does, is it appropriate to name that which calls " God "?

First, then, can we identify this call forward as a clearly distinct aspect of our experience? We can approach an answer by considering again the meaning of freedom for Jesus. The freedom he offered included freedom from the burden of obedience to imposed laws and from the guilt which arises from failure to obey. But in our day as in the early church it needs to be stressed that this freedom was in no sense license. Freedom was not to be gained by relaxing the existing requirements in favor of the desires of the individual. On the contrary, one became free from the power of existing institutions including moral laws by living toward and out of a new and far more demanding reality.

Most men throughout the subsequent centuries have failed to grasp the distinctiveness of this kind of freedom. Much of Christian history is to be read as a vacillation between new legalisms and rebellious rejections of inherited laws in the name of the individual's right to pursue his private happiness. Many psychological and sociological analyses of human experience in our day also miss the distinctive kind of freedom offered by Jesus in the name of God. Thinking in crudely naturalistic categories, many moderns understand man as torn between the mores inculcated by social teaching and expectation on the one hand and his own individual desires and needs on the other. For them, " law " represents the social requirements and " freedom " means assertion of the desires and needs of the self even when this conflicts with what has been demanded. In such an analysis there is no place for the call forward.

What we are seeking, therefore, is just what this analysis omits, those dimensions of experience which are determined neither by social pressure nor by an individual's psychophysical needs and desires.

Consider the concern for *truth*. Much of this is quite simply pragmatic in character. We want certain ends for ourselves, and in order to attain them we need accurate knowledge. Societies inculcate the moral importance of truthtelling largely because of the disastrous social consequences which follow

Yes. This call forward cannot be reduced to psych. terms — like power of sin!

when men lose basic confidence in the word of their fellows. But the power of truth exceeds and ultimately even contradicts this kind of motivation. We inherit a tissue of beliefs from the past which fix a context within which our desires are structured. We become accustomed to these beliefs and they provide us a basic security. We believe, for example, in the essential virtue of our nation's international policies or the American way of life. We know that radical criticism is profoundly threatening to our self-esteem and to our established habits. And of course we know how passionately men and nations have struggled against learning a truth that would shatter their self-image. Nevertheless, there is also in us, alongside the desire to gain our personal and social ends, an experience of the claim of truth, whatever its emotional and practical consequences may be. The call to expose our received and established convictions to ever-new criticism and evidence is one aspect of the call forward of which I am speaking. Hopefully most men can identify it in their experience and recognize its distinctive power over against the social and personal pressures more often regarded as " natural."

The call forward can also be recognized in the power of *disinterested concern* for other persons. In our relations with those with whom we are in close interaction this element of experience is hard to distinguish. We know how much of our concern for these persons is based on our desire for their good opinion of us or our enjoyment of their company, and psychological analyses have tended to interpret our concern for others as an extension of our self-love. Yet it is possible to attend to just that element in one's relation to other persons which such analyses fail to capture, the element of *disinterested* concern.

To focus attention upon this element in experience, one can consider his attitude to persons remote from himself, persons whose lives will not impinge on his, or whose interests may even conflict with his. Does genuine concern for such persons exist? The question is not whether concern for them is strong in comparison with self-interest or with feelings about family and friends. Few could claim that. Nevertheless, behavior is misunderstood when we neglect this factor of genuine concern for others apart from the consequences for ourselves. At least some men do care, although not nearly as much as we could wish, about what happens to a Chinese peasant in a village of which they have never heard. The cynical explanation of all altruistic action as motivated by some self-seeking goal is inadequate to the reality of human experience and behavior, although on the other side, anyone who supposes that his motivation is purely or even primarily altruistic needs to recognize how complex are the factors that lead to action. My argument is not that anyone is ideally altruistic or even dominated by altruistic concerns. My argument is only that the need of another human being does lay a claim upon a man, which is independent of social mores and private desires.

The point I am trying to make is a simple one, yet one that is easily overlooked and that runs counter to many prevailing tendencies. We tend to think that human behavior is caused by antecedent conditions. These conditions are recognized to include motives and purposes, but if these in turn are explained by antecedent conditions, they must finally be displayed as grounded in fundamental biological and psychological needs and drives. In this way one can account both for conformity to social mores and for rebellion against them. Thus the present and future are viewed systematically as outgrowths of the settled past. A complete determinism on a mechanistic model is the usual and consistent consequence; or, if the determinism is restricted, this can only be in favor of chance.

As a guide to some kinds of research this model may be a useful one, but even for the psychologist its inadequacy is becoming increasingly apparent. As Abraham Maslow notes, " In recent years more and more psychologists have found themselves compelled to postulate some tendency to growth or self-perfection to supplement the concepts of equilibrium, homeostasis, tension-reduction, defense and other conserving motivations." (*Toward a Psychology of Being*, p. 21.) Maslow does not believe psychologists are yet able to speak with precision of this "pressure toward fuller and fuller Being" (p. 151), but he points for corroboration to the disparate work of such writers as Fromm, Horney, Jung, C. Buhler, Angyal, Rogers, G. Allport, Schachtel, and Lynd (p. 22). Collectively they have shown decisively the inadequacy of interpreting all human action as the effort to satisfy determinate needs and drives.

We may hope that the psychological research models of the future will take account of this crucial factor, but whether they do or not, lived experience includes it. In real life the causal influence of the past is continuously confronted by multiple possibilities for the future. The present is the meeting ground for past and future, the place of anguish and decision. The decision may be to let the causality of the past be all-determinative. If so, the ruts of habit and custom become deeper, and life relapses into meaningless repetition, or, if patterns of expectation on the part of others change, the individual passively accommodates to them. But a man *can* decide against his past habits and against social pressures, not simply as rebellion against them, but as responding to the claim of truth, of the neighbor, or of some ideal possibility. Then life means growth, freshness, and intensification.

Although the claims of truth and of the neighbor are only examples of what meets the causal influence of the settled past in the present, they are typical examples. They are typical in their ideal or normative character. The causal agency of the past is quite sufficient to account for deceit and, of course, for much of our truth-telling. But the experienced claim of truth goes beyond such conditioning as does the claim of the neighbor's need. The ideal and normative possibility for our self-actualization stands in tension with the power of the past and seeks to lure us beyond what the past would otherwise determine for the present. It is this claim of the normative possibility upon us which I am naming the call forward, and this call

forward is the aspect of human experience in relation to which
we as Christians have reason to approach the question of God.

Before we can raise directly the question of God, we must
consider the second major question of this chapter. Does the
experience of the call forward indicate that there is *something
which calls,* some reality to be distinguished from the experience itself as well as from the social structures and human experiences which constitute our past world? A positive answer
to this question would not by itself allow us to speak of God,
for such a reality might be too abstract or too impersonal to
be named " God." But a negative answer would foreclose the
question, for if the call forward is *simply* an aspect of human
experience, it could point to nothing beyond itself, hence, certainly not to God.

Among the influential writers who have recognized the reality and importance in human experience of the call forward
is John Dewey. He describes it as " the power of an ideal." It
will be instructive to see how he understands this power. When
we speak of the power of an ideal, we seem to be attributing
some independent status to it. Dewey speaks of the " *active* relation between ideal and actual " (*A Common Faith,* p. 51),
and he even goes so far as to say that this may be called " God."
In such expressions he seems to suggest that ideal possibilities
have a power in themselves, and in some sense he surely wants
to say that the ideals act upon men. However, his general
philosophical position does not allow him to give them the
autonomy they need to function in this way. He must interpret
them as nothing more than generalizations of features of the
actual, and the activity in question is that of " the idealizing
imagination " which " seizes upon the most precious things
found in the climacteric moments of experience and projects
them " (p. 48).

We cannot take time for a close analysis of the position
Dewey has taken here. He himself, clearly, was profoundly
drawn by ideals to which he gave deep commitment. In his

polemic against certain traditional religious views he emphasized the importance of recognizing that these ideals are not
already existent, and that they should not be projected into an
already actual supernatural sphere. In this he was surely correct. The power of the ideals is to guide us in new fragmen-
tary and partial realizations of them, not to assure us that they
are somewhere else already realized. But having rejected the
existent actualization of the ideals, he was left with a view of
ideals as *projections,* which cannot explain the power he was
concerned to emphasize. The claim of truth or of the needs of
other persons upon me cannot be adequately understood as a
projection. And although my dream of world peace and brotherhood may indeed be a generalization of fragments of peace
and brotherhood I have known, its power resides in its ideal
character objective to me and not in my projection of it. Somehow the ideal must be recognized as having its ideal character
given for me and as coming to me from beyond myself.

Less well known than Dewey, but more penetrating in his
reflections upon the power that calls us forward, is Henry Nelson Wieman. Wieman sees that man tends in each moment to
absolutize the good he has achieved, and thus to obstruct the
growth of new goods which at that point he cannot foresee or
understand. Even his ideals, insofar as they are received from
the past, can function to block rather than to foster growth.
The process that bears man forward is the one in which men
come to entertain new ideals rather than the abstraction and
projection of already experienced values. This process is far
less conscious, less intellectual, less voluntary, than Dewey
suggests. It works in us and among us already in infancy, for
it is the process of human growth itself. It works through the
creative interchange among persons in which each is transformed in ways which none can foresee or control. Awareness
of this process as " the source of human good " calls forth
commitment to it and the willingness to subordinate all existent goods to it.

How can these understandings be incorporated into the ecumenical movement which really rests on already (common doctrinal) actualized ideas?

52   GOD AND THE WORLD

Wieman's expansion of our horizons from the refined levels of experience of which we have been speaking heretofore to a process that includes these as an extreme limit is important and illuminating. Once we have seen that we are drawn by the power of ideals and the claims of others, we can see that there is a similar kind of forward movement much more pervasive of our conscious experience and that this is continuous with unconscious personality growth as well. The movement forward which is highlighted in the special features of conscious experience we have discussed is the process of growth itself which is always a breaking out of established patterns into new possibilities.

Although Wieman's analysis of the process of creative interchange in which all genuine growth occurs is exceedingly valuable, it too has its limits. While he describes this process as a power operative among us quite different from determination by the past, his philosophical stance, being similar to Dewey's, does not allow him clearly to locate this power. His more careful accounts of the process reduce to descriptions of the kinds of situations in which growth occurs and actually say nothing about the cause. Wieman's contribution is chiefly his careful analysis of the process in which man can continuously be reconstituted through creative interchange. But the power that is present in the process to distinguish it from being simply the outworking of the past in the present is unclarified.

When we have seen that the call forward in conscious experience is continuous with the total process of growth in human personality, we are prepared to recognize that this process in its turn is continuous with that of growth throughout nature, indeed with life itself as it has been embodied in the whole evolutionary process. The evolutionary vision of the world has recently been renewed for us in the work of the Jesuit paleontologist, Teilhard de Chardin. In even more vivid and powerful imagery, although of course with far less scientific accuracy, it is captured in the following quotation from the modern Cretan writer, Nikos Kazantzakis:

Blowing through heaven and earth, and in our hearts and the heart of every living thing, is a gigantic breath — a great Cry — which we call God. Plant life wished to continue its motionless sleep next to stagnant waters, but the Cry leaped up within it and violently shook its roots: "Away, let go of the earth, walk!" Had the tree been able to think and judge, it would have cried, "I don't want to. What are you urging me to do! You are demanding the impossible!" But the Cry, without pity, kept shaking its roots and shouting, "Away, let go of the earth, walk!"

It shouted in this way for thousands of eons; and lo! as a result of desire and struggle, life escaped the motionless tree and was liberated.

Animals appeared — worms — making themselves at home in water and mud. "We're just fine here," they said. "We have peace and security; we're not budging!"

But the terrible Cry hammered itself pitilessly into their loins. "Leave the mud, stand up, give birth to your betters!"

"We don't want to! We can't!"

"You can't, but I can. Stand up!"

And lo! after thousands of eons, man emerged, trembling on his still unsolid legs.

The human being is a centaur; his equine hoofs are planted in the ground, but his body from breast to head is worked on and tormented by the merciless Cry. He has been fighting, again for thousands of eons, to draw himself, like a sword, out of his animalistic scabbard. He is also fighting — this is his new struggle — to draw himself out of his human scabbard. Man calls in despair. "Where can I go? I have reached the pinnacle, beyond is the abyss." And the Cry answers, "I am beyond. Stand up!" All things are centaurs. If this were not the case, the world would rot into inertness and sterility. (*Report to Greco,* pp. 291–292.)

It would be idle to expect from the poet-novelist Kazantza-kis an explanation of what he terms the Cry more adequate than the accounts Dewey and Wieman render of the more limited phenomena they treat. The clarification of the call forward as it functions in man's consciousness, in his total growth, and in the totality of nature was the peculiar achievement of Alfred North Whitehead. Whitehead saw that all growth requires the achievement of a novel concreteness. The introduction of novelty requires the confrontation of each situation by the realm of pure possibilities, the reality of which precedes man's experience. The achievement of concreteness requires that these possibilities are so ordered as to be relevant to the actual situation of each becoming entity. This ordering, too, is given for man and not projected by him.

Since, with Wieman, Whitehead understands the growth in question as far wider than consciousness, the confrontation is by no means limited to consciously entertained possibilities. Even in consciousness the sense of the tension between what is and what should be is far more extensive than the intellectual comparison of consciously entertained ideals and the consciously analyzed situation. Each moment of experience in its entirety is the self-determining outcome of the meeting of the energies and forms derived from the past with new possibilities for present achievement. The past requires of each experience that it be somehow reenacted or conformed to. Here is the power of conformity that determines the vast repetitiveness of things. But the ideal exercises also its power upon the becoming experience, calling it to be something more than merely repetitive, and offering it the possibility of achieving some novel synthesis out of all that it receives from the past. There are of course consciously held and long-lasting ideals, but much more important in Whitehead's analysis is the immediately relevant possibility we confront consciously and unconsciously in each moment calling us forward. It calls us so to actualize ourselves in that moment as to embody some ideal maximum of experience which is at the same time compatible with the realization of values by other occasions of experience in our own future and in the wider world. Just what this optimum experience will be can never be described in general, for it is always radically individual, suited only to that person in that time and place.

Whitehead's analysis allows us to understand what both Dewey and Wieman are saying without the curtailments which their philosophies impose upon them. We can see that it is indeed the unrealized ideal possibilities which act upon us, as Dewey says, without undercutting the point by treating these possibilities as mere projections of the human imagination. They come to man with their own self-authenticating quality. At the same time we can recognize that the conscious entertainment of such ideals is a very limited feature of the forward call, and that, as Wieman argues, this needs to be seen in its continuity with the whole movement of human growth. However, whereas Wieman's presentation is limited to a description of the process in which such growth occurs, Whitehead can explain it in more encompassing terms. Thereby Wieman's sense that this process is a power in itself distinct from man and from the determinisms of the past is given full force.

Furthermore, Whitehead's analysis allows us to set what both Dewey and Wieman are saying in the context of the comprehensive vision of Kazantzakis. In less dramatic but more coherent form it explains how the Cry is to be understood as the claim of new, relevant possibilities throughout the domain of life.

We are thus offered a vision of something beyond ourselves and our past that calls us forward in each moment into a yet unsettled future, luring us with new and richer possibilities for our being. That something is an ever-changing possibility which impinges upon us as the relevant ideal for each new moment. It is the power that makes for novelty, creativity, and life. Its power is that of an ideal, a power which is not coercive, but not, for that reason, ineffectual.

Although Whitehead offers us an exceptionally adequate

and comprehensive conceptuality in which to state with some precision the common truth of Dewey, Wieman, and Kazantzakis, this does not mean that his own writings embody all the insights of each. There is, for example, a valid emphasis in Kazantzakis which is only partly to be found in Whitehead. Kazantzakis perceives the Cry or call forward as terrible and terrifying. Whitehead also knows that at times the situation is such that the best that is offered us must appear as oppressive fate. But Kazantzakis means more than this. He sees how passionately each thing wishes to continue essentially as it is, whereas the stability, the happiness, and the security it enjoys are shattered by the Cry. The new into which one is called may afford rewards of its own, but these cannot be foreseen or imagined by the one who is called to let go of what it has. As Wieman shows so clearly, one must abandon the goods he knows, not only out of prudent calculation that greater goods are in store, but in commitment to that process in which new goods arise. Kazantzakis names that process the Cry, and he expresses with poetic power the cost in anguish and suffering by which the creation moves, in response to that Cry, into new triumphs and joys. The Christian too knows that within history, between the pains and pleasures of the life that is given and the triumph and joy of resurrection, for individuals and communities alike, there lies crucifixion. The call forward is toward intensified life, heightened consciousness, expanded freedom, more sensitive love, but the way lies through the valley of the shadow of death.

Thus far in this chapter we have taken two steps in line with the first two of the questions formulated above. First, we have noted that in our experience there is both the causal influence of the past and the fresh claim of newly recognized normative possibilities. This claim we have designated the call forward. Second, we have considered briefly the thought of some men who have recognized the power of this call forward, and we have seen that their accounts, intentionally or unintentionally, witness to a certain objectivity of that which calls.

We are now ready to approach the third and final question of the chapter. Is it appropriate to name that which calls " God "? The question arises especially because the power whose objectivity has thus far been affirmed is only that of relevant ideal possibilities. These are abstract and diverse, whereas we can properly speak of God only when we refer to a unitary actuality. If we carry the analysis no farther, we should hesitate to speak of God, even though Dewey, Wieman, and Kazantzakis all sometimes do so.

Given the climate of contemporary thought and the extreme hesitancy about affirming the actuality of any entity other than those we can identify immediately in our experience, many will want to stop with this stage of the argument. If they are persuaded that the course of nature and human growth at every point witnesses to the incursion of novelty and the power of some relevant ideal, that will be something, for the awareness of this process makes possible an openness to the reality of the dynamic and free elements in the world alongside the mechanical and repetitive. And they may be encouraged to throw the weight of their lives and thoughts in this direction.

My own view, however, is that what calls us forward has the unity and actuality as well as the worthiness of worship and commitment which warrants our use of the word " God." I am not proposing to try to prove that God exists. Rather, I will only indicate some of the considerations that I find persuasive and that led Whitehead also to think of God in much the way here proposed.

Our account thus far has led to the view that the forward movement or creativity of the world involves the meeting in each moment of the settled facticity of the past and the relevant possibilities for the future. Out of this meeting emerges the new actuality. Our question now is, should we seek behind the experienced relevant possibilities the activity of a unitary actuality that confronts us with these possibilities, or can we attribute whatever agency is required to the possibilities themselves?

The difficulty with attributing the requisite agency to possibilities is that in their own being — as merely possible — they are abstract. Platonic philosophies have often attributed to forms or ideas a superior reality such that agency in the course of worldly events might be attributed to them. But even in Plato this is obscure, and the course of philosophy has overwhelmingly militated against the attribution of superior reality or of capacity for agency to possibilities as such. I share with most modern philosophy the view, called by Whitehead "the ontological principle," that only what is actual has agency. Hence, if possibilities unrealized in the past world have effective relevance for new occasions of experience, this is by the agency of something actual.

Not only is that which functions as agent actual, it is also individual. For practical purposes we may speak of the action of a group, but ultimately this action must be attributed to individual members. Therefore, the agency by virtue of which possibilities gain effective relevance, like all agents whatsoever, is an individual or unitary actuality. Since we have attributed cosmic functioning to the call forward, that which calls is best understood as universal in scope and everlasting in duration.

However, even if one accepts the need for thinking of a unitary actuality of cosmic scope mediating to us relevant ideal possibilities, he may still resist calling this agent "God" on the grounds that it does not inspire him to worship or commitment. Since the functions we have ascribed to this agent are eminently important ones, the hesitation is best understood as stemming from the coldness of the conceptuality rather than from the intellectual denial that what calls us forward is worthy of devotion.

The word "God" has connotations of personality, will, purpose, and love which this language about a unitary and actual agent does not. Christians know that the richness of this language about God grows out of a history of human experience with God and cannot be captured by philosophical analysis or reflection on our present experience in separation from the tra-

[handwritten margin note: It may be best to shift to a utility argument at this pt. and note the benefits to individuals of thinking about god (that which is finely based conception) in personalised terms.]

dition. Nevertheless, we can from the side of philosophical reflection take one more step toward bridging the gap. We can ask how the agency that is required to understand our experience in its cosmic context is best conceived, and we may do so by reflecting on the kinds of entities which have agency, that is, the power to act.

We might try to think of an agent as a material entity. But this will not do. The more clearly we limit ourselves in thought to what would be merely material, the more clearly we realize that at best it must be entirely passive and incapable of agency. We might try to think of an agent as a law or principle, but that will not do either. Laws or principles, like possibilities, are abstractions. They are generalized accounts of how things behave, but as such they are not agents causing things to happen in this way. We might try to think of an agent as a force, and here we are surely closer. But we must ask what a force is. Sometimes we mean by a force the flow of energy itself, sometimes we dimly conceive of something acting upon the flow of energy, forming or changing it. Certainly the agency that calls us forward is some kind of force, but our minds cannot rest in that vague notion.

We have seen that agency can be attributed only to unitary actualities, and we are now prepared to assert that such actualities must always be understood to be something for themselves as well as exerting influence on others. That means that every individual actuality is a subject of experience as well as an object to be experienced by other subjects. This point will be discussed more fully in the next chapter. For the present, I simply assert that the unitary actuality of cosmic scope and everlasting duration that in every moment confronts us with new ideal possibilities for our existence is a subject, a center of experience in itself, to which the attribution of personalistic language is not unintelligible.

Before engaging in the more philosophical reflections of the next chapter, we shall here take note of an existential issue — the " So what " question. In our day not only are there all kinds of objections to belief in God, there is also a sincere perplexity as to why so much heat has been associated with the discussion. Many view the use or nonuse of " God language " as a peripheral matter. They are concerned only with what occurs in human history and hence are indifferent to the existence or nonexistence of God as something transcendent to that history.

Many theologians have encouraged this indifference, intentionally or unintentionally, by stressing that God's will is fulfilled in loving service to the neighbor rather than in the direction of energy or conscious attention to God. No wonder, then, that those who hear them conclude that it is the love and service that are important and not their identification as God's will. Furthermore, many theologians have rejected ontological categories for thinking about God, insisting that only historical and existential ones are appropriate. No wonder that their hearers are no longer able to see any reason for referring to the historical and existential phenomena in question as " God."

Unless " God " refers to something whose actuality is *independent* of man's experiencing it, but which nevertheless *affects* man's experience, there can indeed be no reason for deep concern about the use of the word. I have argued that the word does have this kind of referent, and that the referent is supremely worthy of worship and commitment. Even so, the "So what" question must be faced. Suppose there is such an actuality. Does it not function in relation to man whether or not man knows it? Is not the outcome of true worship and commitment to it the same as that of goodwill to fellow human beings? Why, then, carry the extra baggage of questionable beliefs?

A traditional — and still objectively valid — answer to such questions is that, if God exists, then *he* constitutes that which is supremely important. The significance of the human and historical is to be determined in relation to God, and not vice versa! But this answer is not sufficient for those who are convinced of the importance of man and indifferent to everything else. They are asking about the importance *for man* of

belief in God as the One Who Calls, and their question must
be taken with utmost seriousness. Even in the limited space
available here, the beginning of an answer must be attempted.

Each man's life is oriented around something, or some
things. In the immeasurable complexity of his conscious and
unconscious experience he attends to some elements and not to
others. The language he learns profoundly influences this se-
lectivity of attention, and new modes of attentiveness in their
turn influence the language. Of all the words that influence
the direction of attention none is more important than "God."
The word is indissolubly associated with a claim of importance. If "God" is used, as is so often the case, in association
with inherited rules or present mores, attention is focused on
them and their claim upon the present. If "God" is used with
primary reference to peculiarly religious or mystical elements
of experience, attention is focused on them and their claim.
If one heeds the claim, one may cultivate, in the first instance,
his sensitivity to the implications of the rules or mores; or, in
the second instance, the religious or mystical elements of his
experience. Such cultivation in the context of this kind of direction of attention is a major aspect of worship. Of course,
where "God" is used in these or other ways, he may be rejected, but unless that rejection occurs in the name of "God"
understood in another way, it tends to lead to the emptying
of experience and life of an integrating orientation and a sense
of ultimate importance. This can be avoided only if some other
concept, such as nation, justice, freedom, or humanity functions as equivalent to God.

Thus far I have suggested that the serious use of the word
"God" plays a major role in the orientation of life and the
determination of the elements of experience which gain prom-
inence. If so, the naming as "God" of the One Who Calls us
forward has profound importance insofar as it encourages attention to certain aspects of experience rather than others.
The believer in God so understood attends to the sensitization
of his psychic life to the claim of new possibilities and of his

neighbor rather than to inherited rules or religious feelings. In a community of faith he can improve his capacity to distinguish the call of God from the myriad other claims arising within and without. The relative weighing of the aspects of his experience is thus altered. One experiences guilt, not in the recognition that his acts are in conflict with past laws or socially approved patterns, but in the recognition that his bondage to the past and conformity to human expectations have inhibited his response to new possibilities of growth and service.

But do not many persons achieve the same result by rejecting the concept of " God " altogether and orienting their lives toward ideal ends? Yes, but also, No. Certainly many who reject "God" are far more sensitive to the call forward than many who affirm "God." Indeed, as I have emphasized, "God" has functioned all too much to sanction what is given and all too little as the One Who Calls. But if we compare commitment to ideal ends with commitment to God as the One Who Calls us forward, we can see that there are inner weaknesses in the idealist's stance which indicate that belief does matter. The one who dedicates himself to ideals does so out of the correct judgment that these ideals have objectivity to him, that they lay a claim upon him. Yet he can hardly provide for himself an intelligible explanation of how this is so. If he rejects God as the ground of their claim, then he is driven toward describing them — with Dewey — as projections. If one concludes that the value of justice lies not in itself but only in his projection of value upon it, the intensity of his concern for justice is likely to decline or, at least, to be difficult to communicate to others. The sense that justice is an inherently worthwhile goal remains, but when it is *believed* that the value of justice depends solely on the belief that it is valuable, the role of the sense of its objective value declines. If, on the other hand, we believe that the claim of justice upon us is an aspect of the call of God, then our worship of God will include our sensitization to the importance of that claim and to the

It is at this pt. that the "demonic power g sin" also enters. The idea of evil (sure evil) also pts to an external force, we may be called not only to grow but also destruction. Evil is not ong

THE ONE WHO CALLS   stagnation but 63 power
in itself.

concrete relevant possibilities in which the appropriate response can be embodied.

There is much more that can be said. Apart from belief in
God, conscious or unconscious, there is little ground for hope.
Apart from belief in God, the reason for concern about one's
motives and one's responsibility for them becomes obscure.
Apart from belief in God, the claim of the neighbor upon one
can only be understood as arbitrary and unfounded. When belief in the God of the Bible is lost, new divinities of the soil,
of sexuality, of race and tribe arise and old ones reappear, and
the grounds for the prophetic " No! " are gone. Apart from belief in God, history and historical existence become intolerable
and barren and we must fall into a pre- or post-historical existence. All this, and more, I believe with respect to the *importance* of belief, which means, of course, of *right* belief. But
in these chapters this can only be asserted — not explained or
justified.

yes — worse than no belief is destructive belief

In the first chapter, four objections to belief in God, understood as the Creator–Lord of history–Lawgiver–Judge, were
treated at some length. I argued that the traditional approaches to God have little point of contact in the modern sensibility, that they have no distinctive grounding in Jesus
Christ, that they lead to doctrines which make God responsible
for evil, and that the resultant imagination tends to represent
God as a restrictive and repressive force over against man. It
will be instructive to consider now whether the understanding of God as the One Who Calls us into the new future is
relatively free from these weaknesses. I think that it is.

First, the sense of movement into the open future, while it
still must struggle against reductionistic naturalisms and ration-
alisms which seek to explain everything out of the past, is characteristic of a growing sensibility in our time. As the mechanistic cosmology continues to lose ground, the awareness of this
dimension of our experience can be further heightened, and
we may hope that human sensibility will become increasingly
oriented to the future.

The idea of sin as wrong choice (or projection) is a part of the mechanistic worldview ! It 'explains' human behaviour mechanically.

Second, although the conception of God that is here proposed is not to be attributed to Jesus or to the early Christians, it does have an important continuity with their witness. *Its fundamental import for our experience parallels that which their imagery had for theirs.* In both cases God is understood as meeting man in the present in terms of the future, calling him to embody a new and demanding possibility. Without asserting that the view here presented is *the* Christian way of thinking of God, I may legitimately affirm that it is *a* way informed by distinctively Christian motifs.

Third, the problem of evil does not disappear when we think of God in this way, but it loses much of its force. The world is not seen any longer as embodying an omnipotent sovereign's will but rather as responding ever anew to a possibility offered. That the response is imperfect does not imply the imperfection of what is offered. There is no world that does not reflect the influence of God's past agency, but there is also no world that is the product of that agency alone. The terrible reality of evil is neither denied nor attributed to God. (See below, Chapter 4.)

Fourth, God as understood in this way is not a repressive force but a liberating one. Granted, liberation is not the removal of all constraint or the sanctioning of every mode of selfish conduct. But the limits and burdens of the past are constantly transcended by God's agency. What man is offered is the fulfillment — not of every passing desire — but of his capacities for vital and full life and for spending himself for the lives of others.

Furthermore, when we think of God centrally as the One Who Calls us beyond ourselves to the more that is possible, we need not think that the reality which we designate is in itself a different deity from that which has been known through other aspects of our experience. I made a similar point in the preceding chapter in connection with the five ways of approaching God there designated. I indicated that the Whole may also be the Source of natural order, the Ground of being, the Source of obligation, and the Holy One. The problem arises, not in any one of these designations of God, but in making one or another of these or their combination central. I showed that they have often been combined with certain Old Testament motifs in such a way as to give rise to what can be a humanly repressive understanding of God. If now we understand God fundamentally as He Who Calls us to ever-greater love, life, and freedom, this does not exclude the possibility that he is also in some important sense the Ground of our being. Perhaps we must recognize that it is precisely the call to be something more than we have been which initiates and activates every new act of being by which we constitute ourselves. Perhaps it is just this ever-novel lure that is the Source of the order exhibited by nature and the Ground of our moral obligation. Perhaps that which we meet in the forward call which works throughout the cosmos is nothing less than the all-inclusive Whole. And perhaps the sense of the holy derives from our encounter with just this Whole.

If so, and I myself believe all this, then our concern must not be to deny the holy Creator–Lord of history–Lawgiver–Judge but to understand him rightly. Instead of seeing the reality revealed in Jesus in terms of a predetermined concept of transcendent and omnipotent deity, we must reinterpret deity in the light of what is given us in Jesus. That means that the Creator–Lord of history is not the all-determinative cause of the course of natural and historical events, but a lover of the world who calls it ever beyond what it has attained by affirming life, novelty, consciousness, and freedom again and again. The Lawgiver is not the source of arbitrary, imposed moral rules, established once and for all from on high, but the establisher of ever-new possibilities of righteousness which both destroy and fulfill generalizations based upon the past. The Judge is not one who, at some future date, will reward and punish in accordance with our obedience or disobedience, but the one who can give us only what we will receive, thereby " rewarding " the responsive with new and richer challenges but " punishing " the unresponsive by the poverty of their new possibilities. The Holy One is not the primordial sacred which

But there doesn't seem to be an ethical component in this. One can be open to new possibilities that are destructive.

transcends and annihilates all separateness and individuality through mysterious and dehumanizing cults, but the immanent-transcendent Ground of life and creativity which calls us ever forward in and through the ordinary events of daily life and the often terrifying occurrences of human history.

NOTE

Much of this chapter has dealt in somewhat varied and vague ways with relevant ideal possibilities and their role in the world. Underlying this discussion is my understanding of what Whitehead calls the initial aim or the initial phase of the subjective aim of an occasion and its derivation from God. I hope the treatment at this nontechnical level is suggestive and even somewhat persuasive, but it is certainly not rigorous. A somewhat clearer statement is attempted in the following chapter, but my serious effort at philosophical treatment is to be found in *A Christian Natural Theology,* Chapters III, IV, and V.

The position taken in this chapter also implies or presupposes that more is occurring in the process of biological evolution than mechanistic categories can explain. At the same time we must recognize the inadequacies of traditional vitalistic and teleological theories. The Whiteheadian understanding of evolution that fits with the understanding of human existence expressed in this chapter has been most fully and carefully formulated by Richard H. Overman in *Evolution and the Christian Doctrine of Creation.*

In this chapter the direction of the call forward has been described in a variety of ways featuring such terms as life, growth, intensity, consciousness, and love. In *The Structure of Christian Existence,* I undertook to describe some of the modes of existence through which man has successively come in response to the call forward. There the occurrence of alternative and even conflicting lines of advance is also recognized, thus greatly complicating the picture.

Chapter 3

THE WORLD AND GOD

In the preceding chapter an approach to affirming God as the One Who Calls us forward was developed in three stages. First, features of our experience which are oriented to the ideal and the possible were highlighted in distinction from the causal influence of the past. Second, the need to ascribe some objectivity to ideal possibilities was urged. Third, it was proposed that this objectivity is best understood when the effective presentation of ideal possibilities is attributed to God. When God is viewed in this way, he ceases to function as the sanction for established rules and achieved goods and is rather the call to go beyond them, whatever their merits may be. God does not hold us back from taking full responsibility for ourselves and our world, but rather calls us to precisely that responsibility. He does not oppose our quest to become more fully human, but is rather the ground of that quest.

This way of thinking of God has much to commend it. It stands with rather than against the restless search of our day.

It is more faithful to what is revealed to us in Jesus Christ. It allows for rational treatment of the problem of evil. It liberates man from repression and channels his energies into a creative future.

But there are reasons for rejecting talk of God to which all of this is irrelevant. There are those who deny that such talk is meaningful or true because they cannot conceive of a reality other than the empirically given plurality of physical things. Whatever else is thinkable is for them abstract, and an abstract God is no God at all. There are others who would be able to think of another kind of reality alongside all of these physical things but can see no *place* for such a reality in their world. There is no longer any " up there " or " out there " where God could be. There are still others for whom the chief problem is that they can see no way in which God, supposing he exists, can be effective or relevant in the world. They may hold, for example, that all experience arises in sense experience and that God can at best be an inference from such experience. If he occurs in experience only as an inference, how can he function as the forward call or in any other way?

This chapter will deal briefly with these three topics: the mode of reality to be attributed to God, his relation to space, and the nature of the divine influence on the world. What is here proposed is developed with greater philosophical precision in *A Christian Natural Theology*. As in that book, the ideas expressed in this chapter are heavily dependent on the philosophy of Alfred North Whitehead. The chapter concludes with a brief discussion of what Whitehead called " the consequent nature of God " and some quotations on the peace which he believed is possible for man only in his experience of God in this form.

The first question is the ontological one. Is there any other kind of reality besides the physical one? If not, God must be either physical or unreal. Since we cannot assert in the ordinary sense that God is physical, the believer in God must affirm some order of reality different from what common sense means by physical.

There are two ways in which we could proceed. We could accept the commonsense understanding of the physical and then show that such realities as thought cannot be understood as physical in this sense. We could then argue that alongside the physical world there is a mental one.

This procedure has a certain merit. All too many textbooks are written as if all reality could be reduced to a naïvely conceived form of physicality. It cannot. The human mind is capable of functions no machine will ever be able to perform, and in our day it is important to make this point again and again.

However, the addition to a naïve notion of the physical of an equally naïve notion of the mental leads to numerous problems which have made themselves apparent frequently in the history of philosophy. Although thought cannot be reduced to physical activities, it is intimately interrelated with them, and this relation is unintelligible if we adopt an ontological dualism which treats mind and matter as two completely different types of reality. Furthermore, if thought is viewed as the characteristic function of mind and sensory extension as that of the physical, the experience of the physical through the senses is neither clearly mental nor clearly physical. Emotion likewise falls under neither heading. For these and other reasons, ontological dualism is profoundly unsatisfactory and cannot be used as a way of understanding God's relation to the physical world, except very provisionally.

A better approach is through a critique of the notion of the physical. This critique was carried out in a purely philosophical way in the eighteenth century by such men as Berkeley and Hume, who demonstrated that we could form no clear notion of what common sense understood by physicality. It seemed to be reduced to sensory impressions alongside an unintelligible intuition that something external to the sensing organism caused these impressions. More recently the physical sciences have supplemented this philosophical critique with an equally devastating one. The apparently solid, inert objects which give rise to our naïve notion of the physical turn out to be composed exhaustively of subatomic entities whose nature is to act and react. These entities *can,* of course, be termed physical, but they cannot be understood as like the bodies we normally call physical only smaller. Hardly any of the characteristics we commonly attribute to a stone — such as its massive endurance and self-identity through time, its passivity, its impermeability — apply to an electron. The electron can only be understood as a *succession of events* or happenings. These events can be viewed as transmissions of energy from past events to future ones. If we ask what they are in themselves, the only answer possible to the physicist is energy. The building blocks of the universe, the things of which everything else is composed, are energy-events.

The dissolution of the physical into energy-events does not solve the question as to how we should think of God, but it should at least cause us to give up the still widely held notion that only what is physical in the naïve sense is real. It would be truer to say that what is physical in the naïve sense is the by-product of the interaction of energy-events outside the body with those that constitute the sense organs. That God is not physical in this way by no means reduces his actuality.

When we conceive the physical as composed of certain types or aspects of energy-events rather than in the naïve way, the question of its relation to the mental is placed in a quite different context. A thought cannot be understood as a physical activity in the old sense, but it can be understood as an energy-event. My act of thinking receives energy from past occurrences in my body and transmits that energy, appropriately modified, to subsequent events. It thus functions in a way similar to the functioning of an electronic event. The older question of the relation of mind to matter becomes the question of the relation of that energy-event which is conscious and in which thinking takes place to those much more elementary ones where there is neither consciousness nor thought. The former cannot be reduced to the latter or regarded as a mere by-product of them, for the event of conscious thinking has its own unity and creativity. But it need not be regarded as belonging to a completely different order of being.

If the general notion of energy-event is flexible enough to include both unconscious electronic events and activities of human thinking, then it might be extended to include God as well. The believer cannot think of God as physical in the old sense, but when we have probed behind the physical to the kind of reality which gives rise to it, we have stripped the physical of most of those properties which once caused us to contrast God's spirituality with it. For example, the individual energy-event is invisible and, in general, not to be apprehended by the senses. (Only where large numbers of these events occur together are human sense organs activated.) The individual event is active, rather than simply passive; it is a subject rather than just an object.

Just as there are specific differences between those energy-events we call electronic and those we call human, so there must be vast differences between human energy-events and the divine. But the problem posed by such differences is quite other than that which is generated when one supposes he has a more or less adequate notion of the physical and that whatever does not conform to that notion must be to that extent abstract. We now see that the physical in that sense is a secondary product of more fundamental processes, and that when we identify these processes, we have arrived at the kind of reality which can include also what we usually call mental and spiritual phenomena. If what is most real are energy-events, and if these are highly diverse in character, then God can be conceived as a very special kind of energy-event.

One thing that all such events have in common is that they transmit energy from preceding events to following ones. In some instances, that which is inherited by the successors is virtually unaltered in the event; in other instances, it is considerably modified. In the former instance we have to do with phenomena which we commonly call inorganic, in the latter with life and mentality. In both instances there is reception from the past, fresh embodiment, and then a completion which gives rise to a new reception in successors. The difference lies rather in the variety of data from the past which can be taken into account, in the complexity in which the diverse data are integrated and reintegrated in the fresh embodiment, and in the element of novelty that sometimes appears in this process.

The term " energy-event" is a quite neutral one. When we think of an electronic event, we imagine it from the outside. We try to conceive visually or otherwise how such a burst of energy might appear to an observer, even though we know it cannot be observed. When we think of a moment of human experience as an energy-event, on the other hand, we think of it from the inside as it feels to itself, for we are thinking of those events which constitute our own existence. If we thought of God as an energy-event in the former sense only, as if his reality consisted solely in his appearance to others, we would be far removed from the Christian God of whom the earlier chapters spoke. But if we think of God as an event in the latter sense, as an occurrence of thinking, willing, feeling, and loving, then we are close to the heart of Biblical faith. Is there any justification for thinking of a divine energy-event as a subject like ourselves rather than in the external way in which we try to think of an electronic event?

I believe there is. Indeed the problem is not that it is improper to think of energy-events as subjects but how we could think of them in any other way. Consider again the electronic event. When we do so, we suppose that its occurrence is something other than our imaginative entertainment of the idea. We want to conform our idea in some manner to what occurs. Our first instinct, to think of it as somehow visible or tangible, we know to be erroneous. What other means have we of conceiving it objectively? We can conceive of it as it impinges upon its successor in the chain of energy-events which we call the electron. But how can we think of that unless we can con-

ceive of the successor in its act of receiving? And if we do that,
then we are thinking of the successor as a subject receiving the
earlier event as its object. In that case we must recognize that
the only way in which we can think of such events at all is
as subjects which become objects for successor events. The alternative is simply not to conceive of them at all, and I mean
at all. We cannot think of " something, I know not what " unless we have some notion of what " something " means. We
can continue to play extraordinary games with symbols and de-
duce predictions about instrumental readings, but we must
then regard the word " electron " as having no referent in the
real world. We can avoid this strange result and overcome the
remaining perplexing dualism of subjects and objects if we
recognize that every individual event or entity is, in its moment of immediacy, a subject, usually an unconscious one,
which then passes into objectivity in the sense of becoming a
datum for new subjects. These data when grouped in certain
large societies impinge upon our sense organs in such a way as
to give rise in our simplified consciousness to the naïve notion
of the physical. Under these circumstances, whatever subtle
difficulties may arise, there is no fundamental reason to hesitate to ascribe subjectivity to God as well.

If the foregoing is sound, then the closest analogue for
thinking of God is our own immediate experience. Of course,
this cannot be a very close analogue. For example, our subjective experience is heavily dependent upon the contribution of
the senses, whereas there is no reason to suppose that God experiences in that way. If, as some philosophers have supposed,
all human subjectivity arises out of sense experience, then,
after all, we have no clue whatsoever to the divine experience,
and even our ascription of subjectivity to God is virtually
empty of meaning.

The foregoing point can also be made with respect to the attribution of subjectivity to electronic events. If subjectivity as
we know it is vision, audition, touch, and so forth, and if electrons have none of these sensory experiences, then it is quite

meaningless to declare that they enjoy a moment of subjectivity, however helpful that might be in solving other difficulties.

But in fact human experience is not fundamentally sensory. Just as it is necessary to go behind what we naïvely call the physical, so also it is necessary to go behind what we naïvely regard as the fundamental givens of human experience. These givens, whether we call them sense data or objects of perception, have been shown by physiology not to be the primitive givens at all; rather, they are highly organized products of the psyche's life arising from its immediate apprehension of quite another order of data.

Let me explain. One of the most widely held assumptions of physicists is that there is no physical action at a distance. But if a particular chair as a complex of sense data or as a perceived object were understood as *immediately* given to me, that would violate this principle in a most remarkable way. Actually there is no evidence whatever for such a violation. The energy-event in which the chair image arises is a mental one occurring somewhere in the region of the brain. It inherits most immediately from cellular or subcellular events in the brain which in turn have inherited from others in the chain that leads to the eye and finally through intervening space to the chair. The chair *image* may be regarded as immediate, but as such it is effect and not cause of the primarily mental energy-event in which it arose. The chair as a *given,* on the contrary, is very complexly mediated and very indirectly determinative of the event.

This means that the fundamental data for the human mind or subject are not physical objects outside the body, but energy-events within the body. The events that we call mental get their content mostly from events in the brain that we usually call physical. No sense organs are involved here; so this experience is not sensory. There is, therefore, in our own experience a basis for conceiving what nonsensory experience is.

One might object that although we can infer the priority of the nonsensory, all of our experience of the external world is at the level of the sensory. This is almost true, since clear conscious experience is overwhelmingly sensory. But even at this level we find adequate evidence of the importance of nonsensory experience.

Consider, for example, the belief in any given moment that there were preceding moments and that there will be future ones. It is doubtful that anyone can ever succeed in radically doubting the reality of past and future. Yet sense experience as such provides absolutely no evidence for either. It is in any moment simply what it is, wholly silent with respect to antecedents or consequents. One may object that he remembers a past and anticipates a future, and that both the past he remembers and the future he anticipates are sensory in character. But even if that were so, it would not alter the point I am making. Neither memory nor anticipation is a sensory relation. If one remembers a past visual experience, the visual qualities may be faintly present to him. If so, he may include them in his present sensory experience. But if he regards them as stemming from a past experience, then he is introducing an element into their interpretation that he cannot derive from present sensory experience, i.e., an awareness of the past as distinct from the present.

Not only our awareness of our past and future, but also our conviction that there is a real world which exists quite independently of our experience of it witnesses to the presence of nonsensory experience. Sense experience as such can give us nothing but sensa or sense-data, and these are given as parts of the present experience. Either we are to regard our indubitable conviction that we are in a real world transcending our experience as an inference for which there is no evidence, or else we must acknowledge that we are bound to that world in nonsensory experience.

Nonsensory experience occasionally manifests itself in striking fashion in what is called extrasensory perception. Extrasensory perception is by no means the basic evidence for nonsensory perception, but it is a peculiarly vivid expression of it.

The prejudice against accepting its reality has been great, but the evidence of its occurrence is greater still, and the time has come for us to try to understand it rather than simply to prove or disprove its existence. Recognition of the primacy of the nonsensory elements in all experience provides the context for interpreting this special form.

Nonsensory elements in human experience are usually on or beyond the boundary line of consciousness. Analysis of conscious experience shows their presence, but it is extremely difficult to focus on them in sharp attention. Most of them are submerged far below the level of consciousness, and it is in this unconscious nonsensory experience that we have our only clue to the subjectivity of such energy-events as electrons.

But when we think of God it would be disappointing, not to say blasphemous, to take such low-level experience as the clue. God, like electrons, must experience in a nonsensory way, but we would not suppose, therefore, unconsciously. Rather, we must suppose that the immediate nonsensory experience, which in man is overlaid and obscured by the vivid consciousness of mediated ones, is for God fully conscious. The best analogy in human experience for reflection on the divine is to be found in memory.

Consider, for example, a vivid recollection of a past experience. That past experience is present in consciousness now almost as if it were reoccurring. Here there is immediate experience of one occasion by another occasion which is grasped in a nonsensory way. Of course, the earlier experience is usually dominated by sensory elements, but that is no hindrance to the analogy. Although we do not think of God as having eyes, there is no reason to deny him the power to enjoy our visual experiences with us.

Let us suppose, then, that it makes sense to think of a divine energy-event which is a conscious subject sharing immediately in human as well as subhuman experiences. We are now ready for the second major topic of this chapter: Where can this energy-event be? Neither the old imagery of " up

there " and " out there " nor the new imagery of " in there "
and " down there " is of much use to us, insofar as it is allowed the spatial connotations which lie upon the surface. We
may, of course, use these prepositions without spatial connotations. That God is "up there" can mean that he is incomparably greater than we are. That he is " out there " may mean
that we experience him at times in his remoteness. That he is
"within " may mean that our relation to him is a profoundly
intimate one. That he is " in the depths of things " may mean
that we find him more really as we go " deeper " into our own
souls. But none of this helps the questioner who wants to know
where, in spatial terms, he can think of God as being.

To such a question there are just two possible answers, answers which are not as different from each other as they seem.
One may say, first, that God is nowhere. The primary import
of this is to deny that God has a place alongside other places
such that one could be closer to him by moving from one place
to another. In this view space is understood essentially in terms
of external relations, whereas God is related to us internally.
Or space is a function of the kind of extension which physical
bodies have, and God is not extended. God as Spirit, it is said,
transcends radically our categories of space and time which derive from sensory experience of a physical world.

There is no religious objection to this understanding of God
as nonspatial, and it is probable that Whitehead himself held
it, but I find it more intelligible to say that God is everywhere.
In the first instance this means, what adherents of the other
view also hold, that God is immediately related to every place,
that there is nowhere one can flee from him. Certainly it agrees
with the first view in the insistence that God is no more at one
place than another and that, when space is conceived visually,
it fails to apply to God. But the visual understanding of space
has been overcome also in physics without the abandonment of
the idea of space in general.

In modern thought space or space-time is not to be thought
of as a fixed receptacle which preexists events. Rather, energy-

events themselves are the ultimate reality. But these events have patterns of relations with each other which can only be described as extensive. These extensive patterns include successiveness and contemporaneity. They can be analyzed into temporal and spatial relations, but in the last resort even this distinction is secondary. Each energy-event is indissolubly spatiotemporal.

Since each event is both a subject for itself and an object for its successors, we may consider how space or space-time functions in these two dimensions. Physics deals with it in terms of the objectification of events in their spatiotemporal connectedness, but the primary reality is the becoming of new events in their subjectivity. For them space-time is important in that each receives the world from a particular standpoint. That standpoint determines the spatiotemporal system in terms of which it experiences past and present and the relative movements of other bodies.

Both those who assert that God is nowhere and those who assert that he is everywhere deny that God is bound to any limited standpoint within the whole of space-time. Those who assert that he is nowhere argue that God in this respect differs from all other energy-events. Whereas all others must occupy particular standpoints within the whole, God occupies none whatsoever and is thus wholly impartial with respect to all. The alternative is the view that God's impartiality toward all is a function of his omnispatial or all-inclusive standpoint.

The chief objection to this latter view is that it implies that the same region of space-time that is occupied by an electron or a human experience is simultaneously occupied by God. That goes against the widely held view that two entities cannot occupy the same space at the same time.

This doctrine has prima facie merit at the level of what we naïvely regard as physical objects. One book cannot occupy the same space as another, and the same holds true of two molecules. If the space occupied by one entity is included in that occupied by another, we speak of the first as a part of the second, as a page is a part of a book, or a molecule a part of a page. But in this case the whole is simply the sum of its parts. If we think of God as related to us in this way, then either God is everything and we are simply parts and pieces, or else we are everything and " God " is simply another name for the sum total of all the parts. In neither case have we a model by which we can think of both man and God.

But all of this presupposes that the entities of which we speak are objects. If we think of subjects, and especially of the one subject we know immediately, the situation changes. My subjective experience has its own spatiotemporal standpoint. In one sense it extends out over the room and through the past as it brings a new synthesis out of the data it inherits. But it inherits these data from a particular spatiotemporal locus. Spatially, this locus seems to include much if not all the brain. There is no reason to exclude this possibility on the grounds that the presence of my subjective experience would exclude that of the electrons or vice versa. The electrons can enjoy their subjectivity from their very limited standpoints within the brain while I am enjoying mine from the more inclusive one. Each has its self-identity independent of the other. As each passes into objectivity it influences the other. The electronic events in my brain influence my human thought and feeling. My human thought and feeling influence some of the energy-events in my brain in ways that lead to specific bodily functioning obedient to my conscious intentions. Thus the events occupying the inclusive space and those occupying the included space act upon each other in complex ways, but they have also their distinct individuality and autonomy. They are independent as well as interdependent.

I have developed this at some length since I believe it offers us our best analogy for thinking of the spatial relation of God and the world. God's standpoint is all-inclusive, and so, in a sense, we are parts of God. But we are not parts of God in the sense that God is simply the sum total of the parts or that the parts are lacking in independence and self-determination. God and the creatures interact as separate entities, while God includes the standpoints of all of them in his omnispatial standpoint. In this sense God is everywhere, but he is not everything. The world does not exist outside God or apart from God, but the world is not God or simply part of God. The character of the world is influenced by God, but it is not determined by him, and the world in its turn contributes novelty and richness to the divine experience.

The doctrine that I am developing here is a form of " panen-theism." It is, in my understanding, a type of theism. But it differs from much traditional theism insofar as the latter stressed the mutual externality of God and the world, with God conceived as occupying another, supernatural, sphere. It differs from pantheism when pantheism is understood to be the identification of God and the world.

Yet, in reality, panentheism is the synthesis of the central concerns of traditional theism and pantheism, and it distinguishes itself from both only in ways that are secondary. The central concern of traditional theism as against pantheism is not spatial separateness of God and the world, and indeed such spatial separateness has been qualified or denied by many who are recognized as theists. The central concern is that God and man be each understood as having integrity in himself. Theism denies both that God is the impersonal whole and that man is a subordinated part. The central concern of pantheism is to reject an external creator outside of and over against the world who manipulates or controls from without and to assert that God pervades the world and is manifest in all its parts. To both of these central concerns panentheism says Yes, while providing a way conceptually to hold them together.

The third question to be treated in this chapter is that of how God is related to creaturely events and especially to occasions of human experience. Specifically, how does God function as the One Who Calls us to turn from what we have achieved to a new and greater possibility that lies before us?

The answer is that by the way God constitutes himself he calls us to be what we can be and are not. He constitutes himself so as to provide each occasion with an ideal for its self-actualization, and it is in relation to that ideal that each human energy-event forms itself. In Whitehead's technical terminology, in its initial phase every becoming occasion derives its initial aim from God. I shall try to make some sense of what this means in less technical language.

Every occasion of human experience begins with a given past. The past includes energy-events in the brain, as well as past occasions of that person's experience. The new experience must take some account of all of these events, which means that all of them affect or influence the new occasion. How they function in this influence depends on what they are, that is, on how they have constituted themselves. If in the past moment I constituted myself as angry at my friend, in this moment I enter into a situation in which that anger is part of the given. I cannot constitute myself in this moment without reference to that anger. Furthermore, there is a strong tendency for that anger to be reenacted in the new moment. Yet there is no strict inevitability as to the fullness of its reenactment. I may, for example, become suddenly ashamed of that anger, and although that does not cause it at once to disappear, it alters its force. Or I may feed the anger by meditating on past grievances. Whatever I do, I am profoundly affected by the way the past occasions constituted themselves, but what I now become is not strictly determined by that.

What I do with the anger is partly determined by the purpose I entertain. If my purpose is to win my friend's support for a project, I will try to swallow the anger. If I have resolved to do him some injury, I may try to intensify it to assuage or overcome the guilt that accompanies my resolution. My purpose, like the feeling of anger, is largely inherited from the previous occasion, but it is not strictly bound by it. The anger may alter the previous purpose. The previous purpose will not lose all effectiveness at once, for the tendency to reenact is too strong for that, but it can be subordinated, even quite suddenly, to another purpose.

The total reality out of which each human occasion arises includes not only the adjacent events in the brain and the past human experiences but also God. Like other events, God influences the becoming occasion by being what he is. He entertains a purpose for the new occasion, differing from that entertained by the previous human experience. He seeks to lure the new occasion beyond the mere repetition of past purposes and past feelings or new combinations among them. God is thus at once the source of novelty and the lure to finer and richer actualizations embodying that novelty. Thus God is the One Who Calls us beyond all that we have become to what we might be.

Clearly, we are not to understand every event as simply the embodiment of the ideal that is offered to it. The power of our own past over us in each new present is immense, not only as mere data to be accounted for but also as ground of our new purposes and projects. It is easier to ignore the lure of God than to overcome the weight of that past; hence the appalling slowness of our progress toward full humanity and the ever-impending possibility that we turn away from it catastrophically. Yet over the longer period we can see that even beyond the willing cooperation of his creatures, God has brought us a long way. And in men of peculiar sensitivity and openness we can catch some glimpse of that finer life toward which God calls us.

At this point I have completed the central course of the argument. In the preceding chapters I displayed a consensus of contemporary theology that God must be reconceived in a way more faithful to Jesus Christ. This way points to God's presence as coming to us from the open future rather than from the settled past. We do find in our experience a call forward into this future. That call can be most adequately viewed as coming from something which offers us in each moment a new possibility for our existence. Reflection shows that this is best understood as God. In *this* chapter I have shown that the affirmation of God which grew out of the previous considerations is more compatible than many suppose with reflection upon reality as it is known in contemporary science and philosophy. I do not suppose that in all this I have *proved* the existence of the Christian God, but I do hope to have shown that the Christian can affirm God in a way that is purified and strengthened by the recent attacks on theism and that is at the same time fully responsible philosophically. The believer has no reason to ask more.

Throughout these chapters, and especially in the present one, I have been heavily dependent on the thought of Whitehead. The mode of relation to God which has been in the center of attention is, in Whitehead's terminology, the derivation by every occasion of experience of its initial aim from God. Whitehead speaks of that in God which is the source of this aim as his primordial nature. But he argues that in God there is also a consequent nature. Just as with every occasion of experience there is not only an influence upon the subsequent world, but also, in its own becoming, the influence of the prior world upon it, so also in God. Not only does God influence every occasion of experience, but also, he is in turn affected by each. He takes up into himself the whole richness of each experience, synthesizing its values with all the rest and preserving them everlastingly in the immediacy of his own life. Even the miseries and failures of life are so transmuted in the divine experience as to redeem all that can be redeemed.

The Christian not only understands his faith as a continual challenge to do and dare, to take responsibility upon himself, and to venture out beyond the limits laid down by the past; he also finds in his faith the grounds for confidence that what happens matters. Regardless of how ephemeral the joys and sorrows of life, his own and those of others, they are not trivial or insignificant. Even if man destroys his planet in the near future, our efforts now to preserve it are not worthless. Because what we are and do matters to God, our lives are meaningful even when we recognize that in the course of history our accomplishments may soon be swept away.

Schubert Ogden in *The Reality of God* builds his case on the deep, underlying confidence that life is meaningful, a confidence he finds also among those who consciously and explicitly deny the existence of God. This confidence bears witness to a relatedness to God, because it cannot be grounded in the merely phenomenal or empirical flux of experience. What happens *really* matters only if it matters ultimately, and it matters ultimately only if it matters everlastingly. What happens can matter everlastingly only if it matters to him who is everlasting. Hence, seriousness about life implicitly involves faith in God.

Whether or not this is to be regarded as in any sense an argument for the existence of God, it does effectively and realistically point up the alternative to Christian faith in God as being, not optimistic secular humanism, but genuine nihilism. The sense of meaning which Western man now struggles desperately to retain has its historic ground in faith in God. For some generations, perhaps, it can survive that faith, but not forever. Whitehead provides us with an adequate reflective grounding for the meaningfulness of life.

Whitehead himself does not speak characteristically of meaning but rather of peace. The last two chapters of *Adventures of Ideas* are entitled " Adventure " and " Peace." In these chapters he rarely uses the word " God," but he is nevertheless speaking of that reality which he elsewhere calls God. The primordial nature of God is here pictured as the love that lures man to adventure. This aspect of God and his relation to the world has been the focus of these chapters. But Whitehead rightly feels that something more is needed for human existence, needed even to sustain the adventure itself, and it is this something else which he calls "peace." It derives from man's dim intuition of the reality of God's consequent nature. Nowhere else in all his writings does he recognize so clearly that what he strives to express stands at the very limits of the expressible. The attempt to translate his tentative expression into my own language would only serve to obscure it. Hence I close with an extended quotation from this moving chapter.

The Peace that is here meant is not the negative con- *Whitehead* ception of anaesthesia. It is a positive feeling which crowns the "life and motion" of the soul. It is hard to define and difficult to speak of. It is not a hope for the future, nor is it an interest in present details. It is a broadening of feeling due to the emergence of some deep metaphysical insight, unverbalized and yet momentous in its coördination of values. Its first effect is the removal of the stress of acquisitive feeling arising from the soul's preoccupation with itself. Thus Peace carries with it a surpassing of personality. There is an inversion of relative values. It is primarily a trust in the efficacy of Beauty. It is a sense that fineness of achievement is as it were a key unlocking treasures that the narrow nature of things would keep remote. There is thus involved a grasp of infinitude, an appeal beyond boundaries. Its emotional effect is the subsidence of turbulence which inhibits. More accurately, it preserves the springs of energy, and at the same time masters them for the avoidance of paralyzing distractions. The trust in the self-justification of Beauty introduces faith, where reason fails to reveal the details. The experience of Peace is largely beyond the control of purpose. It comes as a gift. The deliberate aim at Peace very easily passes into its bastard substitute, Anaesthesia. In other words, in the place of a quality of "life and motion," there is substituted their destruction. Thus Peace is the removal of inhibition and not its introduction. It results in a wider sweep of conscious interest. It enlarges the field of attention. Thus Peace is self-control at its widest, — at the width where the "self" has been lost, and interest has been transferred to coördinations wider than personality. (Pp. 367–368.)

At the heart of the nature of things, there are always the dream of youth and the harvest of tragedy. The Adventure of the Universe starts with the dream and reaps tragic Beauty. This is the secret of the union of Zest with Peace: — That the suffering attains its end in a Harmony of Harmonies. The immediate experience of this Final Fact, with its union of Youth and Tragedy, is the sense of Peace. (P. 381.)

PART II. EVIL, RELIGION, AND CREATION

Chapter
4

EVIL AND THE POWER OF GOD

The reality of evil is sometimes asserted as in itself a sufficient disproof of theism. Theism is understood as the doctrine that an omnipotent and all-good being created the world, whereas the presence of evil in the world shows that its creator cannot be both omnipotent and good.

To respond fully to this critique one should deal with all three of the terms around which it revolves: worldly evil, the divine goodness, and the divine power. Reflection shows that all three are highly variable in their meaning, so that the apparent simplicity of this famous disproof of theism disappears under analysis. But the problem remains. The pain, suffering, injustice, and transitoriness of the world both intellectually and existentially call forth radical questioning about God.

In this chapter only the third of the key terms, "power," will be treated critically. It is my conviction that the proper conception of divine power holds the key to the Christian solution of the problem of evil.

The power of God is one of the main themes of classical theism along with his love, knowledge, justice, and immutability. In the major expressions of this theism, sometimes one and sometimes another of these themes has dominated and served as the basis for understanding the others. Where the theme of power has been prominent, classical theism can be read as declaring God responsible for everything that happens in the exact way it happens. In this case there arises the inevitable and legitimate protest that the evil in the world contradicts the claim that God is perfectly good. It is useless to point in rebuttal to man's sin rather than God's will as the source of evil, for man's acts too are held to be caused by God just as they occur. When this view of God's omnipotence is combined with the Christian doctrine of man's accountability, there arises the monstrous idea that God's justice holds men responsible for sins even though God is himself ultimately their author.

One response to this problem has been to deny the divine omnipotence, to assert that the evil in the world is to be explained by the presence in the universe of that over which God does not have power. This approach has the merit of subordinating the doctrine of God's power to that of his goodness or love, but its results are unsatisfactory. To avoid assigning *any* responsibility for evil to God, his power must be conceived as reduced to the vanishing point. If any significant degree of power is attributed to him, there remains the problem of reconciling his love with his apparent use of that power in our world.

The foregoing comments on the consequences of both the doctrine of God's omnipotence and the theory of his limited power assume that the meaning of power is the ability to determine what is to be and how it is to be. As long as power is conceived primarily in that sense, there can be no satisfactory explanation of the evil in the world that does not reject the power of God. To avoid both seeing God as the author of evil and denying God any significant power, we need a basic reconception of what is meant by power. Such a reconception has been achieved by Charles Hartshorne, who has made it possible for us to articulate clearly an understanding of divine power which has always been implicit in Christian faith. We can approach this more Christian understanding of power by looking again at that alternative view of power which it rejects.

Power has often been understood as if it were measured by the incapacity to resist on the part of that on which it is wielded. The potter exercises upon the clay a very great amount of power in this sense. The clay is equally malleable into any one of innumerable forms, and the decision as to how it is to be shaped is solely that of the potter. Apart from his skills the only limits to his power are the nature of the clay and the quantity at hand. Those eager to glorify divine power have argued that even these limits do not apply to God's relation with the world. In this view God dealt with no given material but rather willed the very clay into being out of nothing. The divine omnipotence is taken to mean that there is only one power, namely God, and that all else is wholly powerless. With such a view God is fully responsible for all sin, and if he chooses to hold his powerless creatures accountable, this adds further injustice to his cruelty.

What is often not recognized is that this view not only slanders the moral character of God but also attributes to him very little power. He is seen as omnipotent in the sense of being the only power there is; but where there is no competing power, omnipotence means little. The power required to lead an army of tin soldiers is given to every child, since the soldiers have so little power to resist, but the power required to lead men is incomparably greater precisely because those who are led retain power of their own. To think of God as more like the potter or the child is to degrade his power. The power that counts is the power to influence the exercise of power by others.

The power too often attributed to God is the power to compel or to force. But in my relations with other people, such as my children, the use of such power is a last resort which expresses my total powerlessness in all ways that matter. Consider, for example, what would be entailed if my relations with my children fell to such a level with regard to their attending school. To compel attendance I would physically have to accompany a child to school and sit with him throughout the day. Meanwhile I could not compel my other children to attend their classes. And of course I could not compel the child to learn anything. By the exercise of this kind of power one can kill, but he cannot quicken. It is indeed a wretched and pitiful form of power, and it is astonishing and shocking that this most inferior of all forms of human power should ever have been a model for thinking of divine power.

The only power capable of any worthwhile result is the power of persuasion. Threat may be an element in persuasion, and this element plays an important role in the New Testament. But if it plays more than a subdominant role, it too tends to destroy rather than to build up. Persuasion need not, of course, be verbal. Most of it is far subtler than that. It does not function primarily by appealing to simple self-interest. It depends rather on relations of respect, concern, and love, and the vision of a better future.

Compulsion can be exercised on others only in proportion to their powerlessness. Persuasion is the means of exercising power upon the powerful. If we are to think of God as exercising any significant power upon our lives, we must think — as surely the New Testament thinks — of the kind of power exercised by a wise and effective parent and not of that of a potter.   SERMON - Use prodigal son in terms of power

If we think, then, of God's power as persuasive power, we may still use the term " omnipotence " if we like, but its meaning is quite altered. It no longer means that God exercises a monopoly of power and compels everything to be just as it is. It means instead that he exercises the optimum persuasive power in relation to whatever is. Such an optimum is a balance between urging toward the good and maximizing the power — therefore the freedom — of the one whom God seeks to persuade.

In this view also God has a certain responsibility for sin understood as willful refusal of the best. If he did not draw us toward an ideal in some tension with our other urges and desires, sin would not arise. We would simply do whatever we, quite simply, wanted to do. But there also would be no growth in sensitivity and no check upon the violent clash of self-interest. If God, who places me into the situation where again and again I sin by resistance to his persuasive power, judged me harshly for my sin, I might still complain against him. But if instead he continuously forgives me for my resistance to him and offers me again in each new moment the best possibility for my fresh realization, then the fact that my sin is a function of his gift is no reason for contempt of the gift or resentment toward the giver.

At a personal level, reflecting on the events that constitute our present history, this understanding of the power of God as persuasion is sufficient to allow us to recognize fully the evil in the world without limiting God's goodness. Furthermore, the resulting view is fully Christian. But when we reflect on the total evolutionary process of the universe, additional problems arise.

If we survey the whole course of cosmic development from the hypothesized " Big Bang " to the present and juxtapose it to the traditional theological doctrine of God's calling the universe into being out of nothing in essentially its present form for the sake of man, we confront so radical a difference that all *ad hoc* resolutions are worthless. There is no reason to suppose that the world once came into being out of nothing, or that any precise goal or unalterable, specific purpose has guided its development. The fact that theologians once thought this way is no reason to think so now.

We can meaningfully think of God as creator only when we combine the understanding of God's power as persuasion with the recognition implied by this understanding of power that God in every moment works with and upon the world that is given to him in that moment. If at any point we imagine God's

Problem: How to conceive of God as Creator
w/out attributing trad. omnipotence.

92   GOD AND THE WORLD

willing something into being in a way not conditioned and constrained by what is already given, it must be wholly mysterious to us why he willed into being a universe so difficult to persuade into the achievement of high forms of order and significant intensities of value. If that is the kind of power we attribute to God, then we must either question his wisdom or his goodness. Most of the traditional attacks on theism in the name of the problem of evil implicitly, if not explicitly, assume this kind of power on God's part.

To reject such an understanding of God's power does not solve all problems, but it places them in a context in which further reflection is possible. We must not ask at any given point why God caused just that world to be. Rather we must ask why, given that world, God seeks to persuade it in the way he does. We must think of God's new act of persuasion in each moment as conditioned by just that world which he there confronts. That world, in turn, of course, reflects the influence of God's earlier persuasion, but it is not identical with what he willed it to be. And the world God will confront in the next moment, although influenced by his present persuasion, will not fully embody even the very relative ideal he offers it now.

If we think of our own cosmic epoch, and it is hard to think of anything more inclusive, then we must recognize that for billions of years the cosmos may have been wholly devoid of life. The possibilities of value in such a world are limited indeed, and even if these were fully realized moment after moment, change would be exceedingly slow. Movement in the direction of any significant values was movement in the direction of life, and so far as we can tell, this movement took place on this planet almost as soon as physical conditions allowed. The appearance of life made possible far more rapid changes, and these in turn on the whole were in the direction of richer varieties of life, more possibilities of intensity of feeling, consciousness, and freedom, in short, of greater realizations of value. We can understand this whole process as response to the lure toward greater self-actualization.

The affirmation that cosmic and biological evolution has moved in the direction of greater value betrays fundamental assumptions which should be made explicit. First, existence as such is good. Second, to exist is to be an experience. Third, experiences vary in richness, harmony, and intensity, and there is more value in those experiences that are richer, more harmonious, and more intense. Fourth, richness, harmony, and intensity are not limited to conscious experiences, but they are greatly heightened by consciousness. Fifth, the role of freedom in the sense of self-determination is roughly correlative with the increase of value. Sixth, questions of moral value apply significantly only to man in his maturity and are by no means the fundamental guide to what is valuable in general. Seventh, value, like consciousness and freedom, is always and only to be found in individual experiences.

In this context the problem of natural evil in the usual sense is not acute. The destruction of living things by earthquakes and volcanoes could have been avoided only by vast postponement of the creation of life until a much higher degree of physical order was attained. But in spite of occasional destructive outbreaks there is far more value in a world teeming with life than in a dead one. And perhaps if life had waited for a safer environment, the only moment when the emergence of life on our planet was possible would have long since been past.

The struggle for survival and the law of the jungle also need not appear as peculiar problems for theodicy. Perhaps we can imagine a world in which such struggle would not occur and can regard it as superior to this one. But we can hardly imagine a time in the development of this world in which such a world was a possibility at hand. The struggle for existence is a part of the means whereby greater values have been realized, and it itself reflects and expresses that fundamental drive for more abundant life which is part of the divine contribution to the evolutionary process.

God's work in the world should be understood as that of

persuading every entity to attain some optimum of satisfaction compatible with the maintenance of an order which enables others also to attain their satisfaction. We have seen that the situation given in every moment constitutes a limitation upon the ideal possibilities relevant to that moment and that, hence, the possibility offered by God is " ideal " only in consideration of those limits. Furthermore, a tension may exist between the attainment of momentary satisfaction of a given entity and its contribution to the order requisite for other entities. Hence, God's persuasion may move *against* some theoretical maximum of immediate satisfaction.

A question here arises with respect to the scope of the environment and future whose benefit is taken into account in the aim of each occasion. One might suppose that God's role would be persuasion in the light of the total cosmic environment. We would then expect that God would lure each entity toward that activity maximally beneficial to other entities, and that the entities chiefly considered would be those capable of the greatest realization of value. For example, one would judge that God would seek to persuade a malarial mosquito to starve rather than to feed upon a human being. But there is no evidence of such an activity on God's part, and the problem of evil recurs at this point in the form of the recurrent destruction of greater values for the sake of lesser ones.

God seems to call every living thing to a self-actualization in which immediate satisfaction looms large. That means that God values intensities of feeling even at the price of endangering harmony and order. In the long run, future entities can themselves achieve higher values only when this risk is taken. The evolutionary process has led finally to man, who is capable in principle of unlimited concern for others; and where this capability is present, God calls for its fullest actualization. But at all lower levels of the hierarchy of living things the capacity for concern beyond immediacy of satisfaction is far more limited. The malarial mosquito is incapable of concern for the man and hence unsusceptible to persuasion to spare human life at its own expense.

Much of the evil in the world results from the incapacity of subhuman entities to be moved by inclusive goals. This does not mean that they seek only immediacy of satisfaction. Individual organisms so actualize themselves as both to achieve some immediate value and to provide for future values — their own and those of others. The behavior of the individual cells in a healthy organism has this double thrust; here the wider society for which provision is made is the organism as a whole. Individual ants or bees likewise display this duality, with the wider concern being the colony. Similar patterns can be found among animals. But the aim beyond individual immediate satisfaction has narrow limits, and the welfare of other organisms, colonies, or species appears to be virtually irrelevant.

In men a boundary is crossed. Because we have the capacity of being influenced in our self-actualization by consideration of others without limit, our actual tendency to follow lower forms of life in the narrowness of our concerns has with us a completely different character. What is "natural" to insects is "sinful" with us. The evil involved when a man seizes immediate satisfaction at the expense of his own future and that of others is qualitatively different and far more terrible than the evil involved when the malarial mosquito feeds upon a man. The capacity of man to inflict evil on his fellows vastly exceeds the combined power of subhuman animals to make man suffer. Our final complaint against God may be that he has made us such that we do in fact destroy one another rather than cooperate in the creation of a better world.

But again we must reflect on what it means that God has made us what we are. Certainly he has done so in the sense that he has been that factor in reality which lured nature toward life, consciousness, maximum intensity, and freedom. Man is the supreme work of God on this earth. But he has not made us what we are, if that means that among all the conceivable forms of being he has directly willed this one into being. If he had done so, we might well complain that freedom and richness of experience are theoretically compatible with a much greater tendency to consider the welfare of others equally with our own. But if we understand the creative work of God as it is considered in this chapter, such an ideal possibility is relevant only as pointing the direction in which we may expect God to seek to draw us, not as grounds of complaint that he has not yet overcome our resistance to his persuasion.

If God is understood as that factor in the universe which makes for novelty, life, intensity of feeling, consciousness, freedom, and in man for genuine concern for others, and which provides that measure of order which supports these, we must recognize that he is also responsible in a significant way for the evil in the world. If there were nothing at all or total chaos, or if there were only some very simple structure of order, there would be little evil — there would instead be the absence of both good and evil. Earthquakes and tornadoes would be neither good nor evil in a world devoid of life. Only where there are significant values does the possibility of their thwarting, their conflict, and their destruction arise. The possibility of pain is the price paid for consciousness and the capacity for intense feeling. Sin exists as the corruption of the capacity for love. Thus God by creating good provides the context within which there is evil.

In such a situation we can understand God's continuing work not only as that of seeking ever-higher values with their accompaniment of ever-greater evils but also in two additional ways. First, God aims at the strengthening of good in such a way that the balance of good over evil will be enlarged. This is the way we experience him as persuading us to build social structures which will embody greater justice and to become the kind of persons who will consider more consistently the wider good in its claims upon us. Second, God shares with us in the suffering that accompanies the existence he has given us. The fundamental risk entailed in the evocation of intensities of experience is one which he not only imposes upon us but in which he involves himself.

The cross has been the symbol of this understanding of God throughout Christian history. But only recently have Christian theologians taken seriously its message that God, too, participates in the suffering of his creatures. Only recently have a few philosophers achieved the long-established religious conviction that God is not only creator and lord but also " the fellow-sufferer who understands " (Whitehead, *Process and Reality*, p. 532). Not only man but also God is victim of man's age-long resistance to the call to love his neighbor as himself.

Since God is to be understood largely as that reality which calls life and humanity into being, the possibility of loving God depends on the possibility of affirming the goodness of life and humanity despite the evils that are involved. He who hates the creation cannot love the creator. But it is equally true that the possibility of affirming life and humanity depends on belief in God. The historic ground for affirming the goodness of creation is belief in the goodness of the creator.

That means that the goodness faith perceives in God is no mere function of the goodness seen in his creation. The highly ambivalent appraisal of man's worth and excellence to which the study of human history must lead is wholly inappropriate in relation to God. The Christian apprehends God as embodying just that purity of goodness for which he searches the world and himself in vain. In worship we praise a divine perfection in which the hungry heart can come to rest, and an indestructible value whose incomparable superiority to all other values makes possible the contemplation even of man's extinction without despair. The Christian loves God finally not as an instrument to human good but for what God is in himself, and that love can make possible the endurance of the terrors of history even when there seems to be no hope for man.

The possibility of confident affirmation of life and humanity in spite of evil depends not only on faith in God, but also on hope. True, even if there is no hope for a better future, it is possible to affirm life and humanity, and hence also the goodness of the creator, even in the face of evil. Yet this affirmation teeters on the edge of an abyss. If, for example, man is destined to destroy his finer sensibilities in orgies of cruelty or to drug himself into a subhuman existence, and if in the end life will fade from the universe leaving no trace behind, then the affirmation alike of creature and creator seems almost pointless. Or if we should project into the future just our kind of world with its balance of love and hate, harmony and conflict, Peace Corps and Vietnam, and suppose that forevermore the world would be like this — and there was nothing more — with how much enthusiasm could we affirm such a creation and its creator? Does not the possibility of wholehearted affirmation depend upon those elements in the present which point at least to the possibility of a better future?

Not only is belief in the goodness of the present world tied up with hope for a better future; so also are faith in God and hope for the future deeply interdependent. If we cannot believe in God, grounds for hope in the future are obscure indeed. If one can discern no hope for the future, then faith in God is in its turn weakened.

The minimum hope that sustains and is sustained by belief in God is that the past is not lost, that achieved value is cumulative. To some extent we experience this in our individual lives. If in each moment we were compelled to begin again from scratch, no significant human experience would be possible. Richness of value in human experience depends on its cumulative character. Even experiences that are in themselves painful or boring can make some contribution to future experiences — even if less than an alternative experience might have made. Some of the most barren or painful moments are endurable because one knows that they too will be taken up consciously and unconsciously into memory. The sadness we feel in the presence of senility and death is largely the sorrow that a rich cumulation of meanings is now brought to naught. Something of this individual's worth is preserved in others' memories, but in the end, insofar as memory depends on man, we must foresee its total loss.

Belief in God adds another possibility. Perhaps our experiences are retained in the divine memory forever. If so, neither individual death nor the extinction of the human race will be so total a loss as it otherwise appears. Even our little virtues and petty triumphs are not ultimately in vain. And perhaps even our meaningless suffering can be subsumed into a larger meaning within the divine life. If all we do contributes everlastingly to God, otherwise ephemeral values take on importance.

There is a second way in which belief in God can nourish hope, thus providing some relief from the horror of evil and supporting the ability to affirm life and humanity. Belief in God is belief that there is a power beyond ourselves which works for good. In " Evil and Unlimited Power," a recent article criticizing the theism of Whitehead and Hartshorne for its inability to solve the problem of evil, Edward H. Madden and Peter H. Hare define theism as belief in that which guarantees the victory of the good in this world. (*The Review of Metaphysics*, XX, 2; reprinted in *Evil and the Concept of God.*) In correspondence the authors acknowledged that this was too strong a formulation, but they maintained that a provisional guarantee of such victory is essential to theism. Even if we reject this view that God *guarantees* the victory of good in this world, belief in God does strengthen hope for man's future. The difficulty of expecting a better future is lessened if there is a trustworthy reality persuading the world toward such a future — even when the contours of that future are now neither visible nor imaginable. I am not able to share the eschatological vision of Teilhard de Chardin, of Pannenberg, or of Altizer. I expect no dramatic reversals or transformations. But I dare to hope that honesty, courage, openness, and the affirmation of life *may* gradually, despite all setbacks, and despite the great power of dishonesty, fear, resistance to change, and hatred of life, lead eventually to a truly better world. I seek no guarantee, either absolute or provisional, but I am sustained by a hope rooted in faith in God.

Here again there is a subtle circularity. If there is no hope for a fuller life and nobler humanity, the affirmation of the life and humanity we know is threatened. If we cannot affirm life and humanity, then there can be no theodicy, and that means that we cannot believe in God. But if we do believe in God, then we can hope. And if we hope, then we can affirm life and humanity. And if we can affirm life and humanity, then the problem of theodicy is existentially solvable, even if we must confess our perplexity about many questions.

Belief that all values are preserved cumulatively in God adds importance to the realization of value, but it mocks me nevertheless at the point at which I care the most. More important than the value achieved is the person himself as a subject of new experience. It is of some importance that the old experiences are remembered, but the pathos is not thereby removed. The pathos is peculiarly acute when we think of a man who gives his life for others, asking no reward for himself. Just because he asks no reward, we feel he *must* be rewarded. If we know of his act, we occasionally honor his memory, but that means nothing to him. There is something rather horrible about believing that for Jesus himself, for example, the cross was simply the end. It is not enough that the values realized in his life are preserved in God or that his memory later awakened faith in others. He knew only that his followers deserted him in the time of his extremity.

Much the same holds also of hope for a better future lying ahead for mankind or for whatever succeeds mankind in the evolutionary development. Such a possibility does add seriousness to the present struggle and give it meaning which partly redeems suffering from horror. But it is not sufficient to still the angry cry. What of all the hundreds of millions who are condemned to perish in the desert before humanity enters the promised land? We who live in comfort and security enjoying rich opportunities for present service and cultural fulfillment may pride ourselves on not demanding anything more of God. But can we equally accept the fate of those whose human aspirations have been thwarted on every side and who have been sustained only by hope? Must we declare their hope delusion? And if so, is not our capacity to say Yes to life and to humanity once again deeply threatened?

If we feel such questions as these keenly, we must reflect seriously on the possibility of belief in life after death, however reluctant we may be to treat this questionable idea. Historically it has played an immense role in the Christian's understanding of himself and of God, and even today we should resist its quick dismissal as a remnant of mythical thinking.

It can be argued against such belief that it has itself militated against the creation of a better world here and now. Undoubtedly a strong case can be made in support of this accusation. But in the longer view, the criticism cannot be sustained. Concern to better man's lot has been more often stimulated than repressed by belief that a man is something more than he appears to be in his brief span from birth to death. The extinction of this belief in something more may temporarily release new forces for revolutionary social betterment, but in the long run it tends to decrease the estimate of the individual's value and to encourage those forces which would rationalize society at the expense of human freedom. Belief that this life is all there is can lead to Auschwitz as well as to socialist revolution, and a revolution based on this understanding of man can introduce new horrors to replace the old.

That belief in life after death need not function against concern for this life is no sufficient justification for its acceptance. Indeed, apart from belief in God there can be no adequate reason for such a hope, and even belief in God entails no assurance. Still, he who believes in God is entitled to hope also in this way. He is entitled to hope first because belief in the divine spirit already implicitly entails belief that reality is not limited to the sensuously accessible world and hence opens up the possibility of belief that there are other spirits as well. And he is entitled to hope also because the God who brought order into being out of chaos, novelty out of endless repetition, life out of subliving nature, man out of subhuman forms of life, and the occasional saint out of a sinful humanity may also have the power to sustain or recreate man in a quite new form. (I discussed the *possibility* of life after death in "Whitehead's Philosophy and a Christian Doctrine of Man," *Journal of Bible and Religion*, Vol. XXXII, No. 3.)

Belief in life after death has often been so conceived as to intensify the problem of theodicy rather than to ease it. Eternal punishment is clearly disproportionate to any human desert, and indeed any idea of retributive punishment, however slight, raises nearly insuperable problems. I can think of God only as offering to each person in each moment of that other life whatever possibility of satisfaction he might attain, just as I see him doing in this life. This does not mean that all would be offered some kind of immediate blessedness there, any more than this is a possibility here. At times the best possible may involve acute pain and suffering, just as in this life the road to fulfillment sometimes lies through agonizing forms of new self-understanding. But it does mean that the image of God's action should be that of the hound of heaven rather than of a moralistic judge.

Belief in life after death, freed from its association with moralistic and punitive judgment, can go even farther than other forms of hope to sustain the affirmation of life and humanity. Even apart from such a hope, we can declare human life good. But only with such a hope can we share in the affirmation that it is *very* good. Here, decisively, belief in God tends to sustain a hope which supports an understanding of the world which in turn resolves the existential problems of theodicy.

Chapter
5

CHRISTIANITY AS A RELIGION

That Christianity is a religion is an assumption so deeply embodied in our ordinary language that it is unwise to attempt to question it seriously. What we ordinarily mean by " Christianity " does come under the heading of what we ordinarily mean by " religion." Some have denied that Christianity is a religion on the grounds that religion is a human activity, and Christianity is a witness to a divine act. However, this ignores the normal uses of the terms involved and should be understood as a proposal for reform not only of language but of Christianity itself. If the denial that Christianity is a religion is based on an identification of religion with a system of myth and taboo from which prophetic faith has freed man, then it must be recognized that Buddhism is not a religion either. Indeed none of the great religions of mankind in their purest forms are " religions " in this sense. But again to say this is quite paradoxical, and such a reversal of normal usage will serve little purpose.

If, then, we assume that Christianity is a religion, there still remains the question as to whether its character as religion is the most illuminating or important thing about it. Perhaps being a religion is only incidental, and perhaps Christianity's chief claim to attention and loyalty arises from features which have little to do with the fact that it is a religion. By analogy, it is surely true that man is a biped. But it is equally clear that we do not come most quickly to what is most interesting and important about man by considering what is common to the class bipeds, including as it does, especially men and birds. If we are interested in man biologically, we will do better to consider him as a mammal, and if we are interested in man theologically, we will do better still to begin with the notion of selfhood or of spirit. My point is, then, that the fact that Christianity does fall under the heading " religion " does not necessarily mean that it is best understood by being approached as a religion. Hence, my major topic in this chapter is determined by the question, To what extent do those aspects of Christianity which demand its classification as a religion lie at the heart of Christianity?

To treat this question I must first attempt some kind of definition of religion. Many definitions are possible, and each is legitimate so long as it is consistently used. Instead of defining it in this sense I shall try to point to several factors which, when they are conjoined, cause me spontaneously to speak of religion. I believe that my reactions here are conditioned by my culture and hence are to some extent typical. When some of these factors are present without others, the question arises as to whether or not I confront religion, and the answer is more or less arbitrary.

The first factor is *concern with a world not given in ordinary sensory experience.* Historically this world has usually included entities superior to man, and the absence of interest in such entities counts against regarding the concern as religious. Nevertheless, when man himself in his deeper reality is understood to be soul or spirit, or at any rate something other than that which is accessible to sense experience, we stand at least on the fringes of religion. We can often see clear marks of religiousness even where there is no belief in a god.

The second factor is a *sense of absoluteness*. For the religious man there is something (or there may be many things) the value or validity of which is not measurable in the endless flux of pragmatic considerations. There is some obligation that does not require justification in any further court of appeal, there is some reality on which everything else depends without being in the same way dependent upon it, or there is some goal the attainment of which transcends the relativity of all other purposes. Probably what I am here calling the sense of absoluteness is inseparable from what is called the sense of the holy, but sometimes the absoluteness is more apparent than the numinous quality of experience.

The third factor is *cultic ceremony* — some more or less standardized form of outward act, private or public, in which the superior reality or power or excellence of something beyond the individual man is acknowledged or celebrated. Usually the cultic ceremony involves some effort to improve the relationship of the individual to the superior reality either by influencing that reality favorably toward the individual or by altering the attitude of the individual, but this is not essential. The cult may be an end in itself.

A fourth factor is an *interest in psychic or spiritual states*. If that which one is seeking to alter is a purely outward condition, we are not likely to think in terms of religion. But when one is trying to attain a psychic or spiritual condition of a sort different from that now enjoyed, he is at least on the fringes of religion.

Where all four of these factors are present and interact and determine each other, I find myself thinking unquestioningly of religion. On the other hand, where only one is present, I am much more likely to view it in other terms. Where two or three occur, I am often unsure how to classify the phenomenon. For example, the first and fourth can be conjointly present in a form of psychology that has affinities with traditional religions without clearly being religious, but if these are combined with either the second or the third factor, I would probably call it religion. Similarly, the second and third factors might be present in a fervent patriot whom we might describe as " almost religious " in his devotion to his country. But if these factors are combined with the first or fourth, I would be inclined to speak of religion. Let us consider now the importance of these several factors for Christianity.

All four are clearly present in historic Christianity. It would be possible to find Christian groups in which one or another played a negligible role, but speaking of Christianity as a whole, we can say that it is clearly religious in the sense now explained. The question is whether in our day, when so much of what has so long been taken for granted is doubtful, we can or should allow a continuing place to these factors. The question is also whether, even if they are allowed a place, this place should be a central one. It can be argued that we are called as Christians to concern ourselves not with an invisible order or reality and special psychic states or cultic acts but rather with the alteration of the social structures which deny to so many people adequate access to the world's goods. Perhaps we are called also to surrender every absolute and to recognize fully the relativity of all our beliefs and goals, including our belief in this relativity. If this is so, then without denying that in fact Christianity has been and continues to be a religion, we should do all in our power to free it from religion. In these directions seems to lie the force of the modern call for secularization of Christianity, although the several advocates of the secular retain different fragments of the factors which, I have suggested, conjointly characterize religion. To come to our own decision on these matters, let us consider the several factors in order.

First, there is the belief in a nonsensory world. That this has been a part of historic Christianity, and indeed an exceedingly important part, can hardly be questioned. Historic Chris-

tianity has concerned itself very much with God, and despite
all the variety of thought about God, there has been virtual
unanimity that God is not directly apprehended in sense experience. The question is not quite so unequivocal when we
come to the understanding of man. On the one hand, the great
majority of Christians have thought in terms of a human soul
that, like God, is not accessible to sense experience. On the
other hand, the doctrine of the resurrection of the body points
to a tradition deriving from the Old Testament that rejects the
idea that what is ultimately important about man can be separated from what is given to the senses.

Assuming that this is a fair statement of what historic Christianity has been, let us consider the case for the secularist. He
will, of course, declare the second element of Christian thinking about man, the one that identifies man as inseparable or
indistinguishable from his body, as the authentic and normative one. With respect to God, on the other hand, he is unlikely to propose that the word be applied unequivocally to an
object of sense experience. Here he can move in two directions. One is to deny the reality or relevance of God for our
present situation. The other, and more moderate, is to emphasize that Biblical thought never directs our concern to what
God is in himself but rather to God's acts in history. These
acts belong to the sphere of what is known by the senses, and
it is this sphere alone which constitutes the proper context for
our reflection and activity. The Christian knows God in the
man Jesus Christ, and hence exhaustively and decisively in
what we can here call secular terms. What he is called to do
in response to this revelation is not to concern himself with
the supposed nonsensory and utterly unknown reality of what
God is in himself but with the empirically given situation in
which he now lives.

Secularization of Christianity in these respects (I do not
here include the atheistic element) has permeated deeply into
the fabric of theological reflection over a period of decades.
We have all learned much from it. Nevertheless, I must reg-

ister my protest against it when it is carried through consistently. It is possible to neglect the question of what God is in himself when everyone has some vague notion of what the word " God " means. But when the word becomes radically problematical, one cannot point to a historical occurrence and say that that is what one means by it. Since this is our situation, we must either give up the word " God " altogether, thereby divorcing ourselves almost wholly from historic, including Biblical, Christianity, or attend to what God is in himself, and that means to his reality precisely as it transcends all that can be apprehended through the senses.

In my judgment the situation with respect to man is parallel. It is well to emphasize the intricate unity of the psychophysical organism that is man as known to modern thought and to show that the Bible too thought in terms of a unity of man rather than a dualism of body and soul. Nevertheless, this emphasis on unity is useful only so long as a part — and indeed the most important part — of that whose unity is asserted is itself not simply body and bodily activity as experienced by the sense organs. As long as this is tacitly assumed, we can emphasize the bodily character of man to our heart's content, but if our hearers really have no notion of any other dimension of man's being, the consequences of the idea that man is *merely* body will be disastrous. Christianity, I am convinced, is *most* concerned about man as self, as " I," or as spirit, and in a sense such that this element cannot be seen, heard, or touched either in oneself or in others.

Second, there is the factor of absoluteness. Christianity historically has involved many absolutes. There have been absolute norms in ethics and doctrines of absolute importance. The human soul has been understood as having absolute significance and heaven or the Kingdom of Heaven has been seen as an absolute state. Finally, God himself has been affirmed as absolute, and that in many senses.

The process of secularization of Christianity has been a process of relativization in all these fields. Contextualism in theological ethics is relativization of natural and positive law alike. At times it seems to maintain the absoluteness of " the law of love " and to that extent to resist full secularization, but it is questionable whether any clear or distinctive meaning can be given to this apparent exception or whether it can survive as an absolute when all else is relativized.

Liberalism, and especially that form of liberalism that has developed out of pietism, has radically relativized all doctrines. It sees what one believes as a function of what one is and the needs one has and not as having real importance in itself. Not doctrine, but one's tolerance toward all manner of beliefs becomes the criterion of health and authenticity. However, there are consciously or unconsciously some beliefs that usually retain an element of absoluteness, and this can be seen in connection with the historic sense of the absoluteness of the individual soul. If we substitute person for soul, we generally find that even the most secularized of Christians affirms something like absoluteness of the individual. Indeed it is often in the name of the ultimate and supraempirical importance of each man that the polemic against other absolutes is launched.

Secularization has gone farther toward the dissolution of an absolute end, whether this is defined in terms of heaven or of the Kingdom of Heaven. Christians have learned to think in terms of an endless process of history or of an end which is in no sense teleological but merely a total destruction. In such a context there is no possibility of the realization of a stable consummation, hence no absolute goal to foresee or work toward. Instead of an absolute good, we are told to seek relative justice in the ever-changing historical situation, recognizing that every achievement paves the way for new distortions with which, in their turn, we must seek to deal.

The relativization of God has proceeded along several lines. One might think of the denial of God's absolute power or control over all that occurs or the emphasis upon the inclusion in his being of the relative events of nature and history. But far more important for our present purposes is another kind of relativization, namely, the relativization of beliefs about him and of his importance for man. This has already been indicated above in the discussion of doctrines. If the many different beliefs about God are recognized as each having its validity relative to the perspective from which God is viewed, then any lingering affirmation of the absoluteness of God loses its force. If these several beliefs are evaluated, not in terms of their truth, that is, their correspondence to the objective divine reality, but rather in relation to the needs of the believer, then the way is open to recognize also in outright disbelief a maturity as great or greater than that found in belief. There is no longer any way of thinking of God as being of absolute importance or reality over against man. Similarly, when God's reality and self-disclosure are understood as having no other implications than that men should seek justice and righteousness in history, and when it is recognized that many pursue these goals without belief in God, then belief in God appears to be expendable rather than absolute.

Once again in these comments I am trying to point a direction rather than to describe a position. It appears to me that religion in its fullest sense involves the conviction that there is something the value and validity of which is not to be measured by any standard beyond itself. This conviction has eroded to a very great degree also within Christendom, and this erosion is properly identified with one aspect of secularization. Whether one can identify Christians for whom no absolute at all remains in this sense is questionable, although it is clear that there are fully secular thinkers for whom this is the case.

Our question is now, To what extent should we affirm and encourage this process of relativization? My judgment is that we should do so to a very large extent and that in this respect prophetic faith does press toward secularization. Against the many restrictions which religion is always inclined to place upon critical inquiry, we must continue to protest in the name of faith. No beliefs, institutions, moral codes, or cultic practices can be regarded as sacred and thus placed beyond such criticism without violation of the fundamental prophetic rejection of idolatry. Even the absolutizing of love and of the human person must be subjected to constant criticism. But in the prophetic tradition all such rejection of the absolutizing of what is not really absolute has been rooted in the absoluteness of God himself. If God, too, is relativized, the result will be either nihilism or a new idolatry.

The relativization of ethics also, despite its indispensable contribution to the necessary dissociation of Christian faith from particular codes, is in danger of ignoring real elements of absoluteness. I suggest that we can divide ethical judgments into two elements, which can be called formal and material. An example of a purely formal principle would be that, all other things being equal, we should treat equals equally. The qualification, " all other things being equal," takes into account the fact that more than one such formal principle may be relevant to a given decision, and in this case there arises another level of consideration as to how to relate the several relevant principles. If the " absoluteness " of a principle means that it could under no circumstances be modified because of the relevance of other principles, then I am *not* now talking about absoluteness. But I am supposing instead that a principle has an absoluteness if it is such that whenever it is relevant it bears an inescapable weight for the moral agent in process of decision. In this sense there is an absoluteness about the principle that we should treat equals equally. The principle remains, however, altogether formal, and no concrete decision could ever be deduced from it alone, for its application depends upon one's judgment as to what is equal. Are monkeys equal to humans? Are children equal to adults? Are men equal to women? Are fools equal to geniuses? Are Chinese equal to Nigerians? Are fish equal to seals? And where there is no equality, what is the degree of inequality? Apart from judgment of material questions of this sort the principle can have no application, and I doubt that " absolute " answers are possible to these questions, that is, answers not subject to further critical reflection. This means that no absolute moral rule is possible, but it does not mean that there is no absolute element relevant to the judgment of the many relative moral rules.

Finally, there is the question as to whether we can as Christians approve and further the dissolution of the hope of a final self-validating state of being. We can generally recognize that there is no such state within history and that Christianity has historically centered much of its concern upon such an absolute state either at the end of history or in a sphere alongside this one to be entered at death. Today a great many Christians consider the reality of such a state exceedingly doubtful and call upon us to fulfill our vocation in this life without reference to any such hope. I myself feel deeply torn on this question. On the one hand, I feel the full force of the skepticism and in fact live my life from day to day with little conscious concern for an ultimate state in some other sphere. On the other hand, I wonder whether the concern for this world, for which we are supposed to be freed by renouncing the next, can indefinitely survive apart from this other belief. This doubt arises from two questions. Can the judgment of the ultimate importance of every human being, on which Christian concern for one's fellowman's well-being in this life is largely founded, survive critical examination when separated from the belief that man has a destiny beyond this life? Can our sense of the importance of service and the quest for justice in the midst of infinite relativity survive the deeply felt awareness that there is no final goal of all our efforts? To me it seems that the understanding of man and of love motivating secular Christians and humanists still feeds on assumptions instilled by centuries of Christian belief in an absolute End.

The third factor I proposed as characteristic of religion is cultic ceremony. That public and private worship have played a large role in historic Christianity is hardly disputable. But the value of that aspect of Christianity is very much subject to dispute. The critique began, long before the rise of Christianity, already with Amos, and those who would now call us out of our churches into the world can understand themselves in continuity with much of the prophetic tradition. The secularization of Christianity would certainly involve at least a de-emphasis of cultic ceremony in favor of involvement in the effort to help men in their daily lives. Thoroughgoing secularization would not necessarily bring about the end of all coming together of Christians for mutual support and encouragement, but the coming together would be for the purpose of making more effective the ministry in the world.

Thus far nothing has been said of the secularizing process that would necessarily do away with worship in the form that we have known. However, if the secularization of Christianity assumes and encourages the secularization of man, then the need to worship would itself be identified as a passing one. Human fellowship, mutual criticism, and exhortation might still have their place in the secularized church, but man would have learned to get along without celebrating the reality of God or directly seeking to improve his relation with God.

What are we to say of the ideal of a deculticized Christianity? Is worship expendable? Most of us would agree that too many Christians have thought of themselves as fulfilling their fundamental calling as Christians by participation in public worship and private devotions. Also, we would have to admit that frequent participation in such cultic acts has not gone far toward Christianizing attitudes and convictions on urgent questions like race relations. Furthermore, the intrinsic enjoyment received from participation in worship seems usually to have more to do with the feeling of self-righteousness than with the objective meaning of what has transpired. Finally, a good many of those engaged professionally in the teaching of Christianity drift away from regular participation in worship and detect no loss as a result. A great deal of evidence can be amassed in favor of the view that authentic faith has little to do with cultic observances.

Nevertheless, I cannot finally support the proposal for deculticizing Christianity. Although it happens with peculiar vividness only rarely, worship is that act in which I am most often and most regularly brought into deeper awareness of the reality in which I believe and of myself as I am in relation to that reality. The reality of which I speak is that both of God and of my fellowman, both of the present and of the past. For professional reasons I think about this reality a good deal, but the realization of it in a prayer of penitence, a hymn of praise, or a preached word that strikes home, is a quite different matter from the critical reflection about it which is my stock in trade. Although the humility, praise, honest self-recognition, and resolve which arise in genuine worship are too often overshadowed by the sense of legalistic self-righteousness that one has attended church, nevertheless, worship remains the fundamental shaper and bearer of Christian existence.

The fourth factor is interest in psychic or spiritual states. This interest has been so extensively taken over by certain forms of psychology, forms which we have learned to think of as quite secular, that it may even seem odd to list this as a characteristic of religion. Yet I think, for example, of the attitudes of a worshiper as more and less " religious " according to the extent to which he is directly or indirectly interested in his own psychic or spiritual condition. And I think of the psychiatrist as performing a priestly, i.e., religious, role in our society. Existentialism too can be seen as playing a religious role for our day. Also when we ask why we incline to classify primitive Buddhism as a religion in spite of its atheism and deemphasis of cult, we turn to its concern for bringing into being a new psychic state. Probably we would not be inclined to understand it as a religion if there were not also a finality or absoluteness about the state sought.

The secularization of Christianity turns attention away from our inner states and our quest for peace of mind or spirit toward the outward work of transforming the world. The Christian's concern, we are told, should not be to save his soul but to help his fellowman. Also the help extended to others is not to be thought of in such subjectivist, and hence religious, terms. This tension between the subjective and objective emphases has been present within Christianity for many centuries, and hence the thrust toward secularization in this sense is far from new. However, in conjunction with the loss of belief in a final judgment, the religiousness has become an end in itself, and hence its repudiation in the name of secularity has taken on new violence.

The extreme dangers of religiousness in this sense are unquestionable. When I was a pastor in the North Georgia Conference, I learned that those most likely to be difficult to deal with were those who announced their experience of the second blessing — sanctification. Also, all too often, those who specialize in prayer, understood subjectivistically, are those who will not take a stand on crucial issues or find time for the acts of service that are most needed. They are content with the warm glow of their own feelings, carefully cultivated in religious devotions.

But all of this does not argue against the importance of subjective states but rather shows the extreme importance of correcting false notions about these states. Although it is wrong to dismiss social activism as an expression of certain immature needs, the effectiveness of action *is* often influenced by the motivation from which it stems. There is a historic Christian wisdom about this motivation which needs to be brought into effective interaction with the wisdom of psychology and existentialism. Christian love cannot be identified with deeds of service, for it is also a peculiar motivation of such deeds. Here too full secularization must be resisted.

My conclusion from the above is that religious elements are of the essence of historic Christianity, that full secularization of Christianity is impossible, and that as a goal it can be destructive of much that is valid and valuable. At the same time, Christianity has benefited immensely and continues to benefit from the process of secularization. It would be just as true, indeed still truer, to say that secular elements are of the essence of historic Christianity, that full religionization of Christianity is impossible, and that as a goal this too would be destructive of much that is valid and valuable. Hence, *the conclusion that religion is an important aspect of Christianity does not determine that religion is the best category for its understanding.* Indeed, none of the great religions is best approached in terms of what is distinctively religious in its constitution. Furthermore, the primary competitors of Christianity are not other religions, but nationalism, communism and anticommunism, and the quests for peace of mind, salvation through sex, and economic security. The reason for being a Christian is *not* that one necessarily is or ought to be religious and that Christianity is the best religion. The argument must be rather that Christianity is truer to reality and/or that it more adequately illumines and fulfills man's ultimate needs, both as an individual and social being.

Chapter
6

IS CHRISTIAN THEOLOGY STILL POSSIBLE?

One of the major achievements of the historical consciousness has been the uncovering of the preconscious determinants of thought. These include elements that are common to man as man, elements that are historically conditioned and characteristic of particular epochs or traditions, and also elements that are in considerable measure the achievement of an individual consciousness. It has become increasingly clear that faith, as the basic determinant of man's life orientation, operates most powerfully and pervasively at this level.

If we are interested in the unity of all faiths, we stress those elements which are common to man as man and see how the variety of myths, ideologies, and religious practices expresses a common reaction to the human problem. If we are interested in studying the distinctiveness of a particular tradition, we study the historically conditioned elements common to those who share in it. If we are interested in the religious geniuses of history, the pioneers of really new achievements of con-

sciousness — those rare souls who seem to stand out lonely
against a background of universal misunderstanding — we
study the individual consciousness.

The decisiveness for faith of an interpretive principle that
operates prior to consciousness has received interesting corroboration in the efforts of British analysts to consider the meaningfulness of religious doctrines. These analysts are among
those who have most conscientiously and successfully undertaken to free their minds (at least for purposes of philosophic
discourse) from all determination by preconscious interpretive
principles. They have schooled themselves in the art of ob-
jectivizing the raw data of experience, that is, of denuding
these data of all the meanings with which personal experience
and tradition have colored them. The hope is that, by doing
so, they can first reach agreement as to what is given and then
discuss in neutral terms what meaning these data really have.
The truth is, of course, that insofar as the denuding process is
complete, no avenue is left by which one may return from the
data to their " meaning."

In discussing the claim that God exists, these analysts discovered that exactly the same data could be employed equally
well to argue for it and against it. All the data could be accounted for on either hypothesis, yet both those who argued
for and those who argued against the doctrine really felt that
their arguments carried a weight beyond mere arbitrariness.
That is, some observers really saw the world as created and
felt driven to the hypothesis of a creator. Others saw the world
as a product of chance and/or necessity and felt driven to deny
a creator. To account for the difference, they coined the word
" blik " to refer to what they regarded as their discovery.

We may smile at the naïveté of the assumption that an idea
which was novel to them is really novel, but we can also ap-
preciate the importance of such an indirect verification of the
conclusions of imaginative historical research. If those who
strive hardest to be loyal to the modern ideal are compelled to
acknowledge that they are helpless, in their own terms, to dis-

cuss the validity of faith claims, we may be confirmed in the assumption derived from a different approach, that this must inevitably be so. Perhaps eventually the analysts will recognize that the metaphysical and ethical problems which they have declared meaningless are also meaningful within the context of a " blik " whose only fault is that it differs from their own. Surely any philosophy, not excluding modern analysis, must be finally understood in terms of the underlying " blik " which determines its presuppositions and its problems.

The term " blik " is too artificial to have a long life in philosophical discourse. On the other hand, the more natural terms that have been used are likely to have developed special connotations which may not fit my intentions here. The German *Weltanschauung* is close to what I want, but too often suggests the product of intellectual activity rather than the initial preconscious interpretation of the data on the basis of which the intellectual structure is articulated. Instead, I will use the expression " vision of reality."

I prefer " vision of reality " to the widely used concept of self-understanding, because the latter term is either too narrow or else misleading. If we interpret the term strictly, we must think of a stage of development in which the self has really become an object of thought. Certainly the study of alternative modes of self-understanding is immensely important, but it is appropriate chiefly for the investigation of modern European civilization. If we mean by self-understanding the way in which the whole is apprehended, whether or not it is perceived as containing or relating to a self, then the term means what I wish to refer to, but the use of the term in this way already expresses a particular vision of the world. That is, from that modern perspective which sees the reality in which I experience myself as living as necessarily *my* reality, self-understanding and understanding of reality can be identified. I would prefer, however, to be free to treat this as one vision of reality among others, rather than as the terminological starting point of inquiry.

Taking, then, as my starting point the decisiveness of man's vision of reality for all experience and thought, I affirm that the distinctiveness of the Judeo-Christian vision of reality lies in its vision of the world as creation. This does not mean that the *doctrine* of creation is a unique possession of this tradition. Other traditions have myths of creation and conceptions of creator deities, but in no other case does the creation idea constitute a fundamental basis for interpreting the world, history, and man's self-hood. In other instances, it is *a* belief about the world alongside other beliefs, invoked for special occasions; something else determines the forms of thought and life and self-understanding.

In the Judeo-Christian tradition, however, the essential truth about the world is that it is created by God. This fact determines what is indubitable and what is problematic. It is itself never problematic. Therefore, it is not constantly repeated as we repeat ideas that we fear may not be accepted. It is not argued for nor defended. The world is simply seen as God's creation, and this vision is the starting point for worship and prophecy alike. Three correlates of the vision are worthy of special notice.

The first of these correlates is a historical consciousness. The distinctiveness of the Jewish consciousness is often conceived in terms of the apprehension of time as linear and eschatological. The relative priority, temporal or causal, between the consciousness of time as linear and of the world as creation, can probably not be definitely established, and we cannot specify the point at which they led to a mode of understanding clearly differentiated from that of other Near Eastern peoples. But we can say that, against the background of the widespread practice of mythical re-creation of the world each new year, Israel, at least after the exile, recognized a once-for-all act of God, long past and unrepeatable, and conceived other events, past and future, as additional acts of God rather than as repetitions of archetypal gestures.

The vision of the world as creation implies, in the second

place, that it is a product of divine purpose and that it belongs to God. Man finds meaning for his life by acknowledging that he belongs to God and can seek his ends only within the scope of God's purpose. So long as this vision of the world remains unchallenged, man does not radically encounter the threat of nonbeing or meaninglessness. He may hate God and rebel against him, but his hatred and rebellion have meaning in virtue of the vision. He may despair of attaining a right relation with God or of fulfilling his role in God's providence, but the despair is a profoundly meaningful one. So long as the vision endures, the modern curse of ennui is impossible.

In the third place, whereas the vision of the world as creation gives meaning to historical existence, it also involves the negation of the self-importance of the world and its history. Whenever creation begins to absorb attention into itself, the same vision that justifies its claim to worthwhileness challenges that claim. For if the world is creation, it is insignificant beside its creator! Compared to him, the world is nothing.

The common Judeo-Christian vision has produced these polar tendencies. Some find in the vision a cause of affirming the world and rejoicing in nature and in historical existence. Some find in the vision a cause of negating the world and prophesying its destruction by the wrath of God. But neither affirmation nor negation is ever total, for the vision of the world as creation simultaneously demands both. In the most enthusiastic affirmation there remains the awareness that the world's excellence is derived from God, who is incomparably more excellent still. In the most sweeping negation "worldness" as such is still affirmed. Only the perversity and corruption of this world are wholly condemned. Creation is to be redeemed, not annihilated. It is the vision of the world as creation that holds together psalms and proverbs, Jewish legalism and Jewish apocalypticism, Paul and the English deists.

The thesis that the vision of the world as creation is decisive for the Judeo-Christian tradition could be justified only by taking, one by one, all the problems and doctrines that have arisen within this tradition and showing that each presupposes and is given its characteristic form by this vision. This is impossible here, but I will take one more important example which modern existentialism has rightly highlighted for us — man's consciousness of himself as a product of his past, who is yet capable at every moment of asserting his freedom from that past by deciding for self-determination. It is my conviction that this self-understanding has been determined by the vision of the world as creation.

The world seen as creation compels me to acknowledge that I am myself the work of God, not of myself, or of blind forces, or of necessity. God's purpose brought me into being and rightfully places a demand upon me. A demand made of me from beyond inevitably conflicts with my appetites and passions. Yet I cannot understand my obedience to appetite and passion as merely natural, for I cannot but acknowledge my Creator's claim upon me. Hence I experience myself as an agent of choice, a will, responsible for obedience or disobedience, transcending both reason and impulse.

As the fundamental significance of my situation becomes clearer, I realize increasingly that my outward behavior, which my will affects relatively easily, is not all that matters. My Creator does not see me outwardly as I appear to the eyes of other men. He knows me inwardly better than I know myself, and what he demands of me, therefore, is purity of purpose or motive as well as the righteousness of overt deed. Since God knows and places a demand upon my inward self, I must become aware of that self as well. All self-consciousness depends upon the consciousness of being known, and that consciousness of ourselves in our depths, that sensitivity to the inner struggles of fear and desire, love of self and concern for righteousness, which is the special product of Christian civilization, depends upon experiencing ourselves as known in our depths, and known by one whose knowledge we cannot ignore because of his rightful demand upon us.

Only when we have discovered the depth dimension of our-

selves, do we grasp the problem of freedom in its most significant terms. We discover simultaneously that we *are* not free,
that those actions which we called free are merely the expressions of habitual attitudes and responses in the inner man, and
that we *can* be free, that we can choose to transcend ourselves
and thus become ourselves.

Whether we view the choice as an act of which man is
capable alone or only by the grace of God is not here the central issue. Whether, furthermore, we follow Sartre in his apparent view that all expressions of freedom are equally good
or whether we follow the Christian view that freedom from
our past is freedom to love and nothing else, also does not, at
the moment, matter. The argument is simply that the discovery of our freedom historically has depended upon the vision
of the world as creation and all that that implies about God
and our relation to him.

The argument thus far has been directed to establishing
two points: first, that the vision of reality is the fundamental
clue to thought and sensibility; and second, that the Judeo-
Christian tradition is radically formed and determined by the
vision of the world as creation. My third point is that this vision is lost to the modern consciousness. This is not to deny
that many people who are more or less affected by the modern
consciousness do *believe* that the world is the creation of God.
I number myself among them. But it does mean that *insofar
as we are " modern,"* formed, that is, by the dominant thought
of the recent past, the doctrine that God created the world has
become exceedingly problematic. Unless we challenge the
dominant modern mentality, we can only justify belief in creation by devious arguments, hold it by an act of will, or accept
it on largely discredited authority. This forces the doctrine of
creation, which has become one doctrine among others, to be
accepted or rejected ultimately in terms of a vision of reality
which is not itself formed by it. The history of modern theology is, therefore, the story of a chaotic plurality of brilliant
but feverish efforts to justify the retaining of one aspect of

Christianity or another, which seems especially precious, in the context of a fundamentally non-Christian vision of the world. In an important sense, no truly modern theology is fully Christian, no matter how great a nostalgia for Christian faith it may betray.

This is not an indictment of modern theologians but a description of the outcome of the situation in which we find ourselves. The major alternative ways in which the finest spirits of our day have faced this situation are profoundly instructive. The responses may be divided first between those who struggle to justify or preserve the creation principle and those who abandon it. Two important examples of the latter choice are Bultmann and Barth.

Bultmann recognizes that " modern " man cannot understand theological claims that involve cosmic activity on the part of God. The cosmos has been radically divorced from our Christian consciousness. That consciousness, however, continues to have some effectiveness in man's interpretation of his distinctively human situation. It is the understanding of this situation, therefore, which must be clarified and proclaimed, and this alone.

Barth, on the other hand, regards God's activity alone as the proper subject for Christian theology. God's activity is always revelation and redemption, and as such *is* Jesus Christ. Hence Christology and Christology alone is the real subject of theology, with all discussion of the other persons of the Trinity essentially incidental thereto. The doctrine of creation ceases to say anything about how the physical universe came into being or what caused man to appear within it, but becomes instead, a subhead under Christology, without actually adding any new element to the discussion.

To deny that Bultmann's position is fully Christian is only to join in a chorus of unsympathetic critics from which I wish to differentiate myself. Insofar as his theology is not Christian, this is because he faces honestly a situation in which Christian theology is impossible. In this lies his strength. His weak-

Creation has been lost sight of:
① Bec. of mod. scientific worldview
② Theol reaction (neo-Orthodoxy) which subordinates "creation"

ness is that he appears to believe that the Christian self-understanding can sustain itself when it is radically cut loose from the Christian vision of the world which gave it birth and nursed its development.

To deny that Barth's position is Christian is to fall into apparent absurdity. Surely he has produced the greatest theological treatise since Aquinas, and surely its controlling principle is the central affirmation of all authentic Christianity. Yet there is a wide gulf that separates Barthianism from historic Christianity. Historic Christianity was a total view of reality within which other areas of knowledge might establish partial autonomy, but within which, nevertheless, all activity and all truth remained. For Barth, Christian theology has as its subject matter, ultimately, only faith as the work of God. Christian faith no longer illuminates anything but itself. Again, as in the case of Bultmann, it is idle to criticize Barth for the tightness of his theological circle. His achievement, too, is a monument to the honesty with which he has faced the contemporary situation. His weakness lies ultimately in the fact that when he has finally succeeded in purifying theology utterly of everything that is not Christ, " Christ " itself must become a word without meaning. The meaning of Christ must be defined either in terms of God, not circularly defined in terms of Christ, or else in terms of the human situation, likewise independently considered. Otherwise, " Christ " simply means certain historical, social, and psychological phenomena which are subject to altogether secular interpretation. In this situation not only is " faith " unable to justify an alternative interpretation of the data; it cannot even intelligibly formulate any such interpretation.

Tillich stands here, as elsewhere, on the boundary — between those who preserve and those who abandon the creation principle. He recognizes as clearly as Bultmann and Barth that modern man has lost the depth dimension of his being, a recognition which I am here regarding as reflecting modern man's loss of the vision of the world as creation. He will not argue

within the context of modern man's vision for belief in the existence of the creator God, nor will he identify God with creative processes within the world as modern man sees them. On
the other hand, he does make God, as the creative Ground of
Being, a subject, indeed *the* Subject of theological discourse.
Translated in terms of what is here regarded as the crucial element of the depth dimension, i.e., a fundamental vision of reality, Tillich's view may be stated as follows: Modern man can
be saved only as his false or inadequate vision is shattered and
healed by the encounter with the Ground of his Being. Life
recovers meaning as it becomes transparent to its Ground, or
in my terms, when the vision of the world (including, of
course, the self) as *creation* is restored.

The difficulty with Tillich's position appears, however, precisely with respect to his conception of God. The belief that
the word " God " has a referent he takes as prior to the encounter with God. That is, God's reality is not proved from the
fact of religious experience. It is rather confirmed by this experience. Neither is its acceptance an act of sheer, irrational
faith. When rightly understood, he claims, " God " is the starting point of reason as well as revelation. Tillich can make this
claim only because he identifies God with Being Itself. That
Being *is* he takes as axiomatic. However, he confronts major
objections on two points.

In the first place, philosophy, rightly or wrongly, has learned
to do without the idea of " Being." The dominant modern vision of reality does not seem to allow a place for such a concept, or at least it renders such a concept problematical. Hence,
the fundamental principle of Tillich's theology is not anchored
in universal reason as he hopes, but in a particular vision of
reality which is no longer dominant. In the second place, if
God is identified with Being Itself, nothing which is thought
about him is either true or false. It is neither true nor false
that he creates the world, has purposes for the world, acts in
human history, redeems men, etc. Hence, the interpretation of
life which in important ways Tillich transmits from the tradi-

tion to the present world cannot be anchored in his under-standing of the relation of God and the world. Indeed it stands in ultimate tension with Tillich's doctrine of God or else is simply meaningless. To put the matter in other terms, the more strictly we press the consistent implications of the doctrine that God is Being Itself, the less intelligible is historic Christian teaching.

These frequently repeated criticisms are somewhat unfair to Tillich, since his doctrine of God is in line with the traditional doctrine from the time of the fathers. Most of the theologians of the church from Augustine to Schleiermacher have affirmed doctrines of God in terms that are subject to criticism in much the same way as is Tillich's. Yet most of them have not been regarded as threatening the Christian faith but rather as defending and supporting it.

In this claim to continuity with the tradition, Tillich is justified. The consistent implications of the doctrines of Augustine and Aquinas are just as destructive of Christian faith as are those of Tillich. However, in their day everyone knew that the God of whom they spoke *was* the creator God, and what is implied about him by the vision of the world as creation was believed regardless of the difficulties of articulation. The radical inconsistencies into which they were plunged were accepted because the common starting point was itself beyond dispute. Today, however, the same verbal statements and philosophical principles, cut loose from the vision of the world as creation, cannot operate as a bridge over which we can return to the doctrines implied by that vision.

The effort to reestablish belief in the doctrine of the creator God within the framework of the modern consciousness has been left largely to the English-speaking world. Two distinctive American approaches are those of the Boston Personalist school and the Chicago Neonaturalist school. L. Harold De-Wolf and Henry Nelson Wieman will serve as suitable living representatives. Both hold that the existence of the creator God is an implicate of rationally ordered experience. Since they both take seriously his function as creative, neither places God in the atemporal realm of Being Itself. Both believe that God is that to which we owe all that is most precious in our lives and to whom, therefore, we are supremely bound in gratitude and adoration. Both, therefore, strive to affirm important elements in the view of God which were implicit in the vision of the world as creation, and both allow their doctrine of God to have a formative effect upon their other religious beliefs. The question is whether, in doing all this, they rely upon a ground for thought and experience which is disappearing from the modern consciousness rather than upon a neutral, universal human experience and reason, as they suppose.

With respect to DeWolf, the answer to the question must be affirmative. For him, the existence of the creator God is not radically problematic. It requires evidence, of course, sufficient to show its probable truth, but the arguments that are advanced are filled with concepts and presuppositions which have become alien to the modern consciousness. They continue to be helpful to those predisposed to faith, who seek to be reassured as to its reasonableness, but serious philosophers outside the Personalist school do not find them persuasive in the form in which they are advanced. When faith has just begun to realize its tension with reason, arguments of this sort may prove effective. Once the chasm between faith and the modern world is vitally experienced, they provide no bridge.

Wieman has accepted the impossibility of bridging the chasm by inferential systems. More than any other major Christian thinker prior to World War II, he took his stand within the modern vision of reality. Within the world as grasped by that vision he has undertaken to point out the divine creativity at work. Within this framework, God cannot be understood as a personal Maker transcending the world, but he can be seen as a Creative Process operative within the world for our good.

Wieman's difficulties, however, parallel those of Tillich. Neither Wieman nor Tillich can satisfy either philosopher or

Christian. The philosopher suspects, and probably rightly, that for Wieman the word " God " or, where he abandons that language, the term " creative event," carries overtones of meaning which are not really accessible within the modern vision. The Christian protests that the creator God must be seen as a purposive maker and a subject of experience, rather than as a nexus of strands *within* human experience. (Since writing these pages I both expounded and criticized Wieman as well as DeWolf, Bultmann, Barth, and Tillich much more fully and precisely in *Living Options in Protestant Theology.*)

Once again it must be emphasized that all these criticisms are intended, not as disparagement of the work of the men studied, but rather as clarifying the current dilemma of Christian theology. The creative energy expended by Protestant theologians deserves more rather than less admiration than it usually receives. They have done much to shake the complacency of the modern consciousness. They have made human existence possible for many. They have kept open avenues of discussion between the church and the world. They have done, perhaps, all that it was possible to do, given the spiritual situation of modern man, and they have clarified that situation for us so that we can face it with utmost honesty.

Given, then, a situation in which Christian theology is impossible because the vision of reality in which it is rooted is gone from the consciousness of modern man, we must raise, radically, the question of our pretense to be Christian theologians — whether professional or lay. At this point, Tillich's analysis is the most profound. We are theologians not because we stand *in* the circle of faith (or, as I prefer to express it, not because we possess the Christian vision of reality), but because that faith (or vision) is for us a matter of ultimate concern. This concern compels us to wrestle with the problems of theology and with the question of theological method. We are able to write various kinds of historical studies, critiques of the work of others, and discussions of the nature of theology, its language, and its relation to other disciplines. In short, the modern man concerned with faith can talk *about* theology and even offer propaedeutic considerations. What is impossible for him in the absence of the Christian vision is theology itself, that is, the straightforward explication of Christian belief as truth.

One reason for passionate interest in the Christian vision and the beliefs associated with it is the horror inspired by the emptiness of the modern vision. But we cannot finally remain Christians *because* we dread the alternative. We can be fully Christian only if we believe Christian teaching to be true; and we can fully believe it to be true only if it corresponds with and fulfills our fundamental vision of reality. This in turn is possible only if we participate in the Christian vision. The recovery of this vision cannot be by an act of will, and furthermore, if that vision is false, we must be mature enough to acknowledge its falsity and to abandon our nostalgia for its apparent blessings. The most fundamental intellectual issue is, therefore, whether the vision is true or false.

In our day, we can best approach the consideration of such a question historically. The most obvious reason for believing the Christian vision false is its progressive disappearance in the face of the growing success of the scientific enterprise. Whatever we are compelled to recognize as incompatible with the more plausible interpretations of the total body of scientific findings we are morally obligated to abandon. If consideration of the history of modern thought shows a necessary relationship between the progress of scientific knowledge and the modern vision of reality, then the Christian vision must be quite simply rejected. If, on the other hand, the loss of the Christian vision and the rise of the modern one were not entailed in the scientific advance, and especially if the modern vision proves theoretically as well as existentially inadequate, then one may work for the overcoming of the modern vision in a new, postmodern one, which might renew essential features of the Christian vision.

Historically speaking, the scientific advances of the seventeenth and eighteenth centuries did not serve to weaken the vision of the world as creation. Indeed, the fundamental scientific hypotheses derived psychologically, if not logically, from the vision of the world as creation and as therefore exemplifying rationality, and the success of such hypotheses tended to strengthen their psychological presuppositions. English deism and the Continental Enlightenment are alike built upon the assumption that the world is creation, an assumption that was experienced as indubitable rather than problematic. The thinkers of the period were far more Christian than either they or we have usually recognized, and, on the whole, their negations are to be taken less seriously than their affirmations. In that context, atheism required the postulate that the rational laws discovered in the universe were immanent in matter. Such a postulate appeared eccentric and, indeed, it is in principle almost unintelligible.

Hume is the first man in whom the modern consciousness triumphed, and the form of that triumph is immensely significant. Hume discovered that the fundamental assumptions of both the science and the theology of his day derived from an interpretation of the data of experience which was not justified by the data themselves. Fundamentally, this interpretation was one which posited a " reality " made up of substantial entities as explanatory of the phenomenal flux. Berkeley had already done away with the reality of things or objects, but he kept the reality of the subject of experience. The world, for him, was composed of subjects only, but these subjects inescapably recognized themselves as creaturely. Hence the Berkeleyan vision of the world still implied the indubitability of the creator.

Hume's rejection of the subject as well is decisive. Experience, for the first time in our era, undertook to interpret itself as self-explanatory, as requiring no cause, ground, or support outside itself. Immediately, the ideas of " cause " and of anything " outside experience " became radically problematical. The phenomenal flux is experienced *as* the world, the only world whose existence is known, and the application thereto of the category of creation is at best dubious, at worst, utterly meaningless.

The vision of reality pioneered by Hume enabled him to raise the most searching questions about the entire inherited faith. He saw clearly that the orthodox identification of God with Being, if taken seriously, was indistinguishable from atheism. He could see this because he could examine the actual content of meaning explicitly assigned to terms without having his sight colored by that vision of a created world within which the identification had been made. Likewise he saw that the rationalist's belief in a personal creator could not be justified by argument or analogy, but was the expression of precognitive convictions.

Hume's own vision probably fluctuated between the modern and the traditional. The modern he achieved in his study and the traditional he returned to for purposes of common-sense activities. In this, too, he foreshadowed the experience of many others through a long period of transition which still continues.

Through the mediation of Kant, the Humean vision passed into German thought and set the stage for a Promethean struggle to save the spiritual heritage of the West. The English-speaking world, however, less prepared for transformation by speculation, awaited the laborious process by which the physical sciences caught up with Hume's genius.

So long as the Newtonian vision of the world could be in any way retained, scientists clung to it with remarkable tenacity. But step by step, through the nineteenth century, its inadequacies became apparent. Events at the phenomenal level could not be explained by the type of reality which was posited as lying behind them. The final blow came from Einstein, who not only destroyed the possibility of further intellectual assent to the Newtonian faith, but proffered a new vision of the world to replace it.

The lesson, however, which the dominant majority of scientists learned from the collapse of the Newtonian vision, was that scientists had no business having visions. Observation of phenomenal occurrences had shown their previous categories for understanding a nonphenomenal reality to be wrong. They regarded these categories which they were now forced to abandon as the only possible ones for conceiving a reality explanatory of the appearances. Hence the idea of reality as such, or rather of a reality distinct from the phenomenal flux, was abandoned as a subject of scientific inquiry.

Such a revolution in the physical sciences might have produced a Berkeleyan rather than a Humean vision if it had not been paralleled by the development of scientific psychology. Just as Berkeley's critique of objective substances was applied by Hume to subjective substances as well, so the physicist's abandonment of a reality behind appearances was applied by psychologists to the human being. Thus, the one discipline, which we might have expected to resist the modern vision of the world as phenomenal only, embraced it most self-consciously and articulately and attacked most vigorously the " common sense " of the tradition.

The first philosophical response to Hume (mediated by Kant) was to accept his vision for the nonhuman world but to reject it for men and the human spirit. This tradition is still dominant in the German-speaking world, most powerfully in existentialism. The second philosophic response (directed to Humean science rather than to Hume himself) was to accept its universal scope and to seek to account within it for the order and possibility of prediction which remained for Hume a mystery. Here I am thinking especially of the various forms of positivism and pragmatism which have dominated the English-speaking world in the twentieth century. Chronologically contemporaneous with both these traditions have been many attempts to achieve a new realism.

If the foregoing account reports accurately as to the historical process by which the Christian vision gave way to the modern, then it is clear that the historic success of the modern vision does not justify any claim as to its cognitive superiority. What we have learned beyond serious doubt is that the vision of the world in terms of which we interpret cannot be justified by analysis of the data which are interpreted, once these data are radically abstracted from the interpretive context. We have also learned that this process of radical abstraction, accompanied by the rejection of interpretation in favor of an ideally objective description, does serve as a fruitful tool for scientific research. We have not been shown whether the Christian view of the world as creation is true or false.

The last statement points immediately to the inescapable circularity of the argument. For the modern vision, the question of truth and falsity is meaningless in this context. In establishing truth claims, we may legitimately consider only the processes of thought and the rules of evidence. True *means* verified, and verification can occur only in the phenomenal world. However, if we assume that there is a supraphenomenal reality, either of self or of object, then we may assert that a conception of that reality is either true or false, even though we recognize that we are unlikely ever to achieve a satisfactory verification in any terms. The question as to the relative truth of the Christian and modern visions, therefore, already violates the modern vision by presupposing that the idea of a supraphenomenal reality is meaningful, although it does not prejudge the case for the Christian vision.

For the Christian believer, little justification for asking this question is needed. Since what the theory of meaning implied in the modern vision excludes is not special doctrines but rather religious questions per se, the man for whom these questions are vital does not hesitate to challenge the finality of the claim of that vision to be self-evident. If we are to justify this challenge to the modern man, however, we face a far more difficult task and must acknowledge in advance that failure is likely. We can argue, I believe securely, that science as a historical enterprise has depended upon convictions about reality that are now called meaningless, but this fact may be acknowledged without being regarded as relevant. To establish our case, we must show that the systematically inescapable presuppositions of contemporary scientific research include ideas which are meaningless apart from a realistic ontology. Great ingenuity is being expended at the present time to prove that this is *not* so, and relatively little effort has been made at a comparable level of sophistication to show, as I believe, that it is.

Establishment of the meaningfulness or legitimacy of questions about reality would be only the first step toward the justification of a postmodern form of the Christian vision. Ontological realism may take many forms, and in its materialist and absolute idealist forms can be found serious competitors to Christianity. Nevertheless, this initial step is the most difficult one. Once we can unconfusedly discuss reality as distinct from appearance, creationism, broadly conceived, is in an advantageous position. Pure materialism can only interpret the world as the product of a fantastically remote chance such that every new discovery of order and direction *should* come as the utmost surprise to the scientist, who should expect instead, moment by moment, a return to total anarchy as vastly more probable. Whatever doctrines one may articulately maintain, such a vision of the world is, as a vision, a remote possibility. Absolute idealism, on the other hand, like all ontological absolutisms, demands that we view all that occurs in the phenomenal flux as equally remote from reality in such a way that no interpretation of it is possible.

If we posit reality at all as a ground for the interpretive apprehension of the data of experience, we must attribute to it implicitly some creative, sustaining, and ordering principle. The plurality of ways in which this has been done is great, and many, if not all, of the traditional ways are now impossible; but features of this vision basic to Christian faith may be recovered.

The crucial issue is that of God as knowing subject. If the brief sketch above of the sources of the Christian self-consciousness is to be trusted, the conviction that I am known by my Creator is of supreme importance. It seems to many quite possible to think in terms of creative and ordering forces in the real world which are nevertheless not conscious subjects. Whether or not the apparent possibility is real, is a question of vital import. I believe it is not, but to develop the argument would be to go beyond the limits of a prolegomenon to contemporary theologizing.

POSTSCRIPT

As noted in the Preface, the foregoing part of this chapter was written some nine years ago. These years have seen remarkable changes in the theological scene — changes that in many ways date the work. Still what has occurred can be understood in part as vindication of the central thesis — that the loss of the vision of the world as creation destroys the context within which Christian theology is possible.

The term " vision," which is extensively used in the chapter, I understood and understand as the precritical, preconscious structuring of the experienced world. My view was and is that this structuring is influenced by critical and conscious beliefs and in turn influences them, but that it functions much more widely than these beliefs. Many persons learn and accept beliefs that are out of harmony with their vision of reality. The vision remains the basis of life-determining convictions in spite of avowed opinions. Nevertheless, eventually the conscious entertainment of such beliefs can alter the vision. For example, the vision of the world as creation could determine the basic attitude of persons toward God and man even when consciously avowed beliefs did not fit with it, but the beliefs in question have gradually destroyed the vision.

Historically, Christian theology has operated in the context of the vision of the world as creation, thereby supporting and strengthening the vision. This vision presents the world including men as having reality and importance in themselves but not of or from themselves. Both the reality and the importance are seen as derivative from God, who alone has being and importance not only in himself but also of and from himself. The decline of this vision raises the question of this chapter, " Is Christian theology still possible? " If theology continues to assume the historic Judeo-Christian vision, it loses relevance to modern man, who neither sees nor seeks a reality other than the phenomena — empirically or phenomenologically given. If it accepts the modern vision as its context, its Christian character becomes problematic.

Barth, Bultmann, and Tillich achieved a delicate balance between the two visions of reality. But this balance has collapsed in recent years to such an extent that the simple criticisms which seemed somewhat needed at the time the chapter was written are today trite and superfluous. Many theologians now try to formulate Christian doctrine fully within the context of the dominant modern vision of reality, and they tend to be much clearer than the previous generation as to the gulf that separates them from historic Christianity. It is much more widely recognized now, than when I wrote, that acceptance of the modern vision requires either the most drastic reconception of God or else the complete abandonment of God-language. Gerhard Ebeling's *God and Word* and Paul van Buren's *The Secular Meaning of the Gospel* are influential expressions of this recognition stemming from sharply different versions of the modern vision.

Even though the drastic consequences of accepting the modern vision are increasingly recognized, only a minority of theologians is prepared to engage in the attempt to renew the vision of the world as creation. A diminishing number do so in the broad stream of the Thomist tradition, and Teilhard de Chardin has attracted attention to his quite special form of the Christian vision. Wolfhart Pannenberg is unusual among continental Protestant theologians in his interest in God's creative work in nature as well as history. I remain convinced that the possibility of Christian theology depends upon renewal of the vision of the world as creation and that the philosophy of Whitehead offers the best channel for this renewal.

My answer to the question that is the title of this chapter is, then, No and Yes. No, Christian theology is not possible if the dominant modern vision of reality is accepted as context and norm. Neither Ebeling nor van Buren, for example, provides a place at which Christian theology can stand. Yes, Christian theology can become possible again when this dominant vision is challenged and replaced. Such a challenge cannot be effective if it is heard as an appeal to retrace our steps to the past. It must come in the name of a possible postmodern vision.

In the years since this material was written I have tried to explain and justify the claim that the Whiteheadian understanding of the world is postmodern in the requisite sense. I have also tried to show that it offers us a new interpretation of the world as creation, which provides an adequate and advantageous context for meaningful formulation of the central affirmations of Christian faith. This task is central to my contribution to what I have called " Christian natural theology." With a different focus and emphasis it is central also to the first four chapters of this book. Such an *understanding* of the world may be able to reform and revitalize remnants of the still effective *vision* of the world as creation. It might even bring into being a new Christian vision for those among whom the old one has evaporated.

BIBLIOGRAPHY

BONHOEFFER, DIETRICH, *Prisoner for God*. The Macmillan Company, 1954. This book was also published under the title *Letters and Papers from Prison* (SCM Press, Ltd., 1953).

DEWEY, JOHN, *A Common Faith*. Yale University Press, 1934.

KAZANTZAKIS, NIKOS, *Report to Greco*. Simon and Schuster, Inc., 1965. The quotation from this book was reprinted in Bishop John A. T. Robinson, *Exploration into God* (SCM Press, Ltd., 1967).

MASLOW, ABRAHAM, *Toward a Psychology of Being*. D. Van Nostrand Company, Inc., 1962.

NIEBUHR, H. RICHARD, *The Meaning of Revelation*. The Macmillan Company, 1941.

ROBINSON, JAMES M., AND JOHN B. COBB, JR., eds., *The New Hermeneutic*. Harper & Row, Publishers, Inc., 1964.

WHITEHEAD, ALFRED NORTH, *Adventures of Ideas*. The Macmillan Company, 1933.

―――― *Process and Reality*. The Macmillan Company, 1929.